THE
TRUTH
ABUT
EQUITY

WHAT IT REALLY IS, WHAT IT ISN'T, AND WHY EVERYONE WINS WHEN WE GET IT RIGHT

by
CELESTE WARREN

THE TRUTH ABOUT EQUITY

WHAT IT REALLY IS, WHAT IT ISN'T, AND WHY EVERYONE WINS WHEN WE GET IT RIGHT

Design and cover art by Peaceful Profits.

Paperback ISBN: 978-1-967587-00-1
eBook ISBN: 978-1-967587-01-8

To my children, Christina and John "Steven"
and to every young person in your generation—

May you come to understand the power of equity,
stand boldly for what is just,
and work to build a world where the barriers of the past
are not the inheritance of the future.

This book is for you—and for the generations to come,
so they may know freedom, fairness, and possibility
without limits.

"Equity is not a destination—it's a commitment and a daily choice. We each hold the power to challenge inequity and uplift those who have been excluded. We don't need to wait for perfect systems, we just need to begin with imperfect courage. The time to act is now, and the responsibility is ours."

—The Author

CONTENTS

Introduction: What If We All Began at
the Same Starting Line?... 1

PART I

Chapter One: So What Is Equity, Anyway? 13

Chapter Two: How Do We Combat the "Equity Is
Preferential Treatment" Misunderstanding? 25

Chapter Three: The Barriers to Change—Why Is
Understanding Equity So Hard? 41

Chapter Four: Why Do We Need Equity
Now More Than Ever?... 61

PART II

Chapter Five: Why is Equity Necessary in
a Merit-Based System? 79

Chapter Six: Is "Fair" Just a Place You Go to Look at
Livestock and Eat Funnel Cake? 97

Chapter Seven: The DEI Continuum—Why Do
We Need Diversity, Equity, and Inclusion?...................... 109

PART III

Chapter Eight: Equity in Action | Education
and Healthcare.. 123

Chapter Nine: Equity in Action | Community
Initiatives and Economic Mobility.................................... 135

Chapter Ten: Equity in Action | Workplace
and Teams 147

Chapter Eleven: The Power to Lead Ourselves,
Your Role in Getting Equity Right.................................. 159

Conclusion: Equity Is How We Move
Forward, Together... 165

Resources 169

Endnotes.. 171

About the Author.. 177

WHAT IF WE ALL BEGAN AT THE SAME STARTING LINE?

THE POWER OF EQUITY: HOW HR FOUND ME

In 1987, I was working as a reporter at WVLK Radio in Lexington, Kentucky. I'd known I wanted to be a reporter since the 8th grade, and I had finally done it. But I soon discovered that, in this industry, 10% of the people made 90% of the money. More than that, the racial and gender pay gaps put me at a distinct disadvantage as a woman of color. My salary was low, and the work effort required of me was high.

Back then, the studios didn't have a lot of money to cover events all over the country, so ABC Radio in New York would hire local reporters as their stringers. Being a stringer was the industry term for freelance reporter—someone who got paid by the story, or in my case, by the sports game.

This meant that in addition to my WVLK Radio gig, I occasionally got the opportunity to cover sports for ABC. When I did, I'd get paid for the two hours I spent covering games for the Cincinnati Bengals, Louisville Cardinals, or

Kentucky Wildcats, which was more than I got paid for the entire week as a reporter in Lexington. But those jobs were few and far between, and it became increasingly difficult for me to make ends meet.

Every few months, I'd have to call home and ask Mom and Dad to help me make rent. I had a full-time job, doing the thing I'd always wanted to do but I started to think—it just shouldn't feel like this. There had to be a better way to make a living doing what I loved. So, I set my sights on TV, thinking surely that would be where the opportunities were waiting.

I landed a job at the local television station in Kentucky, an incredible feat as only 33% of women were television reporters at the time.[1] I thought for sure since I'd made it to TV, that everything was going to change—and that I'd finally be making the big bucks.

It was true; everything *was* about to change. Just not in the way I thought.

When I received my TV contract, the salary was almost *exactly* the same as my radio job. I was stunned, and it knocked me off course. What I thought I wanted from my career path came crashing down around me. I couldn't live on this amount of money. I couldn't live like *this*. *What am I going to do?*

To this day, I remember how I felt in that moment—completely deflated. Getting a TV reporter contract was my dream, but the reality was rushing in fast that I couldn't make ends meet from the dream.

The TV station gave me two days to sign the contract. I thought and thought about it. *If I sign this, I'm going to continue to be in the very same position I'm in. I just can't do it.* On that second day, it all snapped into place for me. *This wasn't my destiny; this wasn't my path.* There had to be more.

I decided to go back to graduate school and wanted to be close to home, so I set my sights on Carnegie Mellon University in Pittsburgh. I figured I could use my background as a reporter and my undergraduate minor in Political Science to eventually end up in DC as a press secretary or campaign manager in the policy scene.

Little did I know that what actually awaited me was a decades-long career in Human Resources (HR) and Global Diversity and Inclusion. At the time, I had never even thought about Human Resources. My idea of HR back then was a little four-foot-nine lady with a tightly wound bun on the back of her head passing out job applications.

No, thank you.

Now, with almost forty years of experience as an HR leader under my belt, I know HR is so much more than what you might think it is. It's organizational design, it's compensation and benefits, it's training and development. It's leadership and change-making in its highest regard. Human Resources found me, and it's a path that's afforded me the opportunity to make so much difference in the world.

It all started with a single application to the School of Urban and Public Affairs graduate program at Carnegie Mellon University.

AN ACT OF EQUITY

In the spring of '87, I was accepted into the graduate program at Carnegie Mellon. Along with my acceptance came a strong recommendation from the school that I take their summer program. They reviewed my transcripts and those of other incoming students, to identify those of us who may not have the foundational courses needed to start the fall semester off on the right foot.

My background was in reporting and political science; I had never taken economics or the foundational courses necessary to thrive in urban and public affairs. This meant I would be automatically behind my peers at the start of the school year. I was thankful to have access to this summer program that was designed to bridge that gap, and help me build the strong foundation I needed to start on equal footing with my fellow students that fall.

This summer program was not a barrier to entry that the school placed on me, but instead, an act of equity. Meaning they saw my potential and, from my application, knew I'd make a great addition to their graduate program. I simply lacked a few courses to give me the proper foundation I needed to thrive. This recommendation to attend the summer program before starting classes was not because of my own failures or any lack of intelligence; it was because the education system I grew up in (and my previous background as a reporter) did not afford me the opportunity to take these courses sooner.

Carnegie Mellon offered me a means to get caught up and finalize my acceptance. The program was designed for students of color who were entering the School of Urban and Public Affairs that year. It was offered to any incoming student who hadn't already taken these classes—for reasons including their socioeconomic backgrounds, previous job experience, or because the schools they'd attended before Carnegie Mellon lacked the curriculum or funding to include the required courses.

About thirty of us attended that summer. We were primarily Black students, Latino students, and Asian students, and we spent the summer studying hard.

I learned so much over those two and a half months, not just about macro and microeconomics (although I learned that too), but about the vast diversity that exists within cultural communities. Although society often defines Latino and Hispanic communities or Asian and Pan-Asian communities as belonging to the same groups, there is so much cultural diversity *within* them. This understanding and knowledge went on to shape my focus in grad school and beyond.

Naturally, my fellow program attendees and I became close. When school began that fall, we all had each other to lean on. Perhaps most importantly, our professors didn't need to worry about anyone getting left behind in class because by that fall, *every* student had the knowledge and foundation required to thrive. It was equity in action.

Our group sat together and diligently took notes, our attention rapt on the professor. After class, a white student stopped me in the hall. *"Hey, how do all of you guys know each other already?"*

I explained that we'd been together all summer working on the courses needed to help us be successful this fall semester. I didn't hold anything back or shy away from the fact that I had needed this extra assistance to be prepared to start the year. I explained that it was not an easy summer by any means, but it was vital to ensure I could keep up.

As a person of color, I'd become familiar with playing at a disadvantage. This was one of the first times I'd actually been given the tools to begin at the same starting line as the rest of my classmates—white, black, woman, or man. I was proud to truly be this student's peer and, as such, perhaps naively, expected to be welcomed with open arms.

What I got from him was very different. I'll never forget how he stared me down as if I'd just stolen something from him. *"Why did you get to do the summer program when I could've used learning support like that?"*

I remember being unable to find the words to formulate a response. What was he talking about? He'd already taken the courses we had spent our summer working towards. He already knew the information that we didn't.

He got to spend his summer at the beach, spending that time however he pleased, and he still walked into class that first day with the exact same knowledge as me. Yet somehow, he felt as if something was being taken from him.

I had been so excited to begin classes and to officially start down my new path. But as I watched this student turn his back on me, his disdain written plainly across his face, I once again felt completely deflated.

I realized that he saw our equitable starting point— each student beginning class with the same foundation of knowledge—as a negative because he perceived it as an opportunity that he'd missed out on. Yet, through his background and the school system he was educated in, he *had* already been given this opportunity.

Through this single perspective of "missing out" and perceived preferential treatment, it would appear as if equity is a dirty word. Today, I understand his reaction and his misinterpretation of the act of equity that was afforded to me and my diverse peers. But at that moment, it felt like he saw me—whether it was because of my gender or the color of my skin—as someone who was not worthy of having something he did not.

As the student walked away, I picked my hope up off the floor and started towards my next class.

THE EQUITY DISCONNECT

Looking back, this moment shaped my relationship with equity. This wasn't the first time I faced discrimination—I grew up as a Black woman in America in the 1970s and '80s, after all. But it was the first time I had stepped into a room on equal footing with peers from all backgrounds—*finally* having been given the opportunities that life automatically afforded others.

It was also the first time I realized that instead of feeling like I added value to the conversation as their equal, those around me perceived my hard work that summer as an opportunity that had been stripped from them.

This is the equity disconnect in action—a fundamental misunderstanding of what equity is and what it isn't. This disconnect halts all of us from moving forward. It has the power to hold back not only our educational institutions but also our organizations, communities, and society as a whole—something we'll be diving into in great detail in the following chapters of this book.

Since then, I've come face-to-face with this disconnect time and time again, where equity is perceived as a negative only because it is so widely misunderstood. I've realized that the term "equity" has been continuously politicized and often given false meaning. For many, the term itself has become a dirty word. This needs to change.

Why? Because equity, my friends, is NOT a dirty word.

In fact, acts of equity are how we build thriving societies. They're how workplaces and communities innovate and provide unparalleled support to their people.

Equity levels the playing field, yes. But it also holds great benefits for marginalized groups *and* for those in the majority—something we'll be diving into in great detail in future chapters.

THE MISSING PIECE OF THE PUZZLE IS *YOU*

While Diversity, Equity, and Inclusion (DEI) is an extremely hot topic at the time of this writing—and an incredibly important one at that—this book will focus on the capital E for *equity* in Diversity, Equity, and Inclusion. Because I believe a clear understanding of this term is needed now more than ever. While some concepts surrounding diversity and inclusion will, of course, be included, equity will remain the primary focus.

For a more comprehensive look into diversity and inclusion, I encourage you to pick up my first book, *How to Be a Diversity and Inclusion Ambassador: Everyone's Role in Helping All Feel Accepted, Engaged and Valued.* It is an incredible resource for anyone looking to play their part in fostering a more equal and just society.

Before we dive in, I want to provide a brief disclaimer about what this book is and what it isn't. The purpose of this book is to educate. My hope is that it will serve as a tool to equip you with the knowledge and understanding to not just listen to the clickbait you see in headlines, but to be able to speak to the truth about equity—and then speak up in moments that call for your voice to be heard. Because equity is not a dirty word, and it is not only for those who have been historically marginalized. When we get equity right, it benefits *everyone.*

You can choose to subscribe to what I say, or choose not to, it is entirely your choice. But from my decades of serving as a Senior Executive leading Global Diversity and Inclusion for a company of over 75,000 employees as well as being a Human Resources Leader, speaking on stages, and fostering connections globally with industry leaders and courageous individuals, I can tell you with confidence that equity is the missing piece to building a better world.

If we don't understand equity, we won't get to a truly inclusive culture; we won't get to true equality. Creating an environment where everyone has access to opportunities— and where there are no barriers or obstacles getting in the way simply because of what someone looks like or how they identify—is the ultimate goal.

It is the vision I hold on to throughout my work as a Global Diversity and Inclusion Leader. I hope to pass the clarity of this vision on to you throughout the following pages. This book is designed to show you how to be a piece of the puzzle in building something better. No matter your background, your race, your gender, or however you identify—you are welcome here.

Whether you –

- hold an executive title at a Fortune 500 company
- are a professional working in education, at a non-profit, at a big corporation, or in a small business
- are a stay-at-home parent, or significant other, looking to better understand the varied tapestry of our world and your role in it

– you are welcome here.

Whether you live in the United States, Europe, Asia, or anywhere else your feet are planted—you are welcome here.

We *all* have a role to play in the equity conversation. Some of you may know a lot about equity already but are open to hearing a new perspective. Some of you may be starting from square one and are wondering why I haven't given you the Webster's dictionary definition yet. (Don't worry, it's coming.)

It doesn't matter where you're starting from. What matters is that you're here. What matters is that you leaned into your curiosity and questions and picked up this book. What matters is that you're willing to be a part of the conversation.

So let's talk.

PART I

PART 1

CHAPTER ONE

SO WHAT IS EQUITY, ANYWAY?

EQUITY: WHAT IT IS AND WHAT IT IS NOT

Before exploring how equity in action can enhance social stability, increase innovation, promote economic growth, and benefit us in both the big and small ways, it's important to first clear up a few common misconceptions surrounding the term itself.

If you've ever heard, or even perpetuated, any of these misunderstandings, that's okay, and that's why we're here. To clear up any confusion, let's banish the equity disconnect once and for all by first talking about what equity is—and what it is not.

MISUNDERSTANDING #1: EQUITY = EQUALITY.

Equality means that everyone—regardless of age, gender, sexual orientation, or ethnic background—receives <u>the same</u> resources and opportunities.

Equality = treating everyone the same regardless of individual differences or circumstances.

Equity is defined as being fair and just in the way that people are treated. This treatment, while free from bias or favoritism, tailors support to individual needs so that everyone can have access to the opportunities they need to thrive.

Equity = actions done to tailor support to individual needs, which enables fairness.

Equity and equality are not one and the same. In fact, they make different assumptions about the way our societies actually work and about our individual contributions within them.

Understanding the difference here is pivotal.

Asking for everyone to get the same thing regardless of real-world factors that come into play—that is equality. Put another way, equality does not inherently take into account the varied places from which we all start. Instead, it asks that everyone be given the same exact resources, no matter their personal circumstances or the things they uniquely need to succeed.

Equity, on the other hand, asks for every individual to be given the resources and treatment they need to thrive. Equity understands that we do not all begin from the same starting line.

It asks us to truly get to know our coworkers, our community members, friends, and family for who they are and what their unique, individual needs are—and then to treat them accordingly.

Equity means fair treatment, access, and opportunities for all through tailored support to individual needs. It asks us to support those who need a boost so that we all can see beyond the barriers that prevent us from contributing our whole selves to the world.

To recap, equality asks that we treat everyone identically, and yet our humanness inherently means we are not the same. While equality is a noble ideal, it is not where we should first place our focus, as it fails to reflect the imbalances and complexities of our current world.

Instead, it is through acts of equity that we transform communities, drive businesses forward, and improve lives on a global scale. When people feel valued, empowered, and even embraced for their beautiful uniqueness, they are able to innovate in truly unparalleled ways—and that innovation has the power to change the world.

MISUNDERSTANDING #2: EQUITY MEANS GIVING PREFERENTIAL TREATMENT.

Over the years, equity has been politicized to mean giving preferential treatment to marginalized groups—specifically people of color, women, those with disabilities, or our LGBTQ+ peers, as examples.

But equity is not about preferential treatment. It is about leveling the playing field so that we can all have our turn up at bat for the same game. It is this misunderstanding that separates our societies, organizations, and individuals from the thriving world that is waiting on the other side of equitable functions.

One of my favorite ways to banish this particular bias is by getting visual. The following equity analogy is one I've used for years speaking on stages across the world, and it has provided so many ah-ha lightbulb moments to those in the audience.

I've had people come up to me and say, "*That's the first time someone has explained equity to me, and I got it*".

My hope is that this analogy will do the same for you here today.

THE EQUITY ANALOGY

The simple truth is that all of us, at one point or another, have had an opportunity that we've taken for granted because we've always had access to it. From childhood to adulthood, this opportunity was a given, inherently ours, and influenced how we navigated the world—and how the world treated us.

Because of this truth, we don't often see our givens as opportunities. We forget or fail to acknowledge that not everyone is afforded the same opportunities or resources. I ask you to reflect on one of your givens that may be seen as an opportunity for another. This might be as small as seeing yourself (people who look like you) represented in leadership or in the shows you watch on TV. Or it may be as significant as access to a good education, or receiving financial assistance for the down payment for your first home.

Now, what about an opportunity that you'd desperately like to have but that, try as you might, you haven't gotten yet because of personal circumstances that are entirely out of your control? An example of this could be as simple as wanting to take more leave from work to care for a loved one, attend therapy, or work on a personal project. But you can't afford to take unpaid time off or lack access to supportive benefits and paid leave.

As uncomfortable as it may be, I ask you to bring that thing you desperately want with you as we explore the equity analogy together. Although it can be frustrating to reflect on the things we want but don't yet have, it will help us all understand the equity analogy through the same lens, but tailored to our individual experiences.

In this first image, it is assumed that everyone benefits from the same support. They are being treated **equally**.

Individuals are given different support to make it possible for them to have equal access to the view. They are being treated **equitably**.

All three can see the view without any support because the cause of inequality was addressed. The systemic barrier has been **removed**.

The image above, from the Deloitte Review,2 is one I've used for years to illustrate the progress of equity. It perfectly illustrates inequitable practices in societies and organizations. While I know there have been other depictions of equity over the years, I am using this one to illustrate my point throughout this book. Let's discuss how this illustration expertly depicts equity in the short term and the long term.

Picture three people, each standing before a fence and trying to see over it. Each person is standing on one rock of the exact same size.

Person #1 can easily see over the fence. They might not even see it as a barrier because they have always been able to see the beauty that lies beyond.

Person #2 can barely see over the fence. Even with her rock, she has to stand on her tiptoes to see just a sliver of what lies on the other side.

Person #3 stands on his rock like the other two. But no matter how hard he tries, he simply can't see over to the other side. The fence blocks his way. Time and time again, his efforts fail to get him any closer to seeing what lies just beyond the fence.

In order to fully understand equity at play, the illustrator gives us a second depiction. One where all three people can now see the same wonder that lies beyond the fence.

Person #1 still stands on the rock they had before, gloriously looking to the other side. But this time, those standing beside him can see as well.

Person #2 has been given a second rock. She can now see over the fence just as well as Person #1.

Person #3 has been given three rocks and can now see over the fence just as well as his peers.

These rocks are acts of equity. They are support tailored to individual needs so that everyone may see over the same fence.

Person #1 always had the opportunity that allowed him to see over. But perhaps more importantly to note is he can still see just as well. Affording an act of equity to his friends did not take anything away from him. He still has the same opportunities as before.

Person #2 needed a little more support to be able to see clearly. She can now see as well as the person on her right *and* on her left.

Person #3 needed the most tailored support, yes. But notice, affording him an extra rock or two did not take anything away from Person #1 or Person #2.

We now have three people who can see beyond clearly— three people who can contribute ideas and unique skills to what lies beyond. Before, they were unable to make this contribution simply because they did not have the rocks (or the foundation) they needed to see over the fence.

THE ANALOGY IN TODAY'S WORLD

This illustration represents what we can build together by putting acts of equity in place. However, in today's society, the person on the left in this illustration turns to his right and on seeing that his colleagues have gotten extra rocks, asks the question, *"Why do they have more rocks than I do?"* Unfortunately, what he doesn't realize is that the fence is there in the first place, because he has always been able to see over it, and it has never been a barrier.

In my analogy, the fence represents all of the systemic issues (problems that affect an entire system—such as the justice system, education system, healthcare system, and financial system) that exist in our present society, issues that take far longer to dismantle. I call these systemic issues the "isms": prevalent long-term barriers like fascism, sexism, racism, etc.

Today, the person who has always been able to see over the fence does not understand that this same fence is a barrier that his peers face every day. He doesn't understand that the fence manifests itself to the individuals to his right in the form of blocked opportunities, microaggressions, and other systemic obstacles that keep them from contributing their best selves to society.

For this reason, it becomes important that we do three things simultaneously:

1. We have to put the acts of equity (the rocks) in place <u>while</u> we tear down the fence. The rocks of equity are our short-term solution to a larger problem that will require a much longer time to solve.

2. We need open communication with the individual on the left to help him understand what it's like for his two colleagues who face obstacles on a daily basis.

3. With help from the individual on the left (the person who has always been able to see over the fence) as an active ally, we can get to the third illustration, where no rocks are needed, the fence is torn down, and everyone can see the beautiful mountains ahead.

Yes, the ideal here is that there is no barrier, no fence at all, to block anyone from the opportunities they seek. That everyone, no matter how they identify, is able to step forward with no needed support.

But the reality is, we're just not there yet. Every country, big or small, was built upon systemic issues that prevent this ideal. There is a lot of work to be done before we're able to smash those barriers and break down the obstacles that stand in our way.

This is why equality is a brilliant idea in a perfect world. But also why it is through necessary acts of equity that we can hope to move the needle forward towards equality *today*.

THE EQUITY ANALOGY IN ACTION

Remember the story I shared in the introduction? I was given a rock of equity through the summer program at Carnegie Mellon. This rock allowed me to see over the fence to begin classes that year with the same vantage point as the rest of my peers.

Had that student—who felt as if I'd taken something away from him by attending the program—understood the equity analogy, my hope is that he would have had a very different takeaway.

In that particular scenario, he was Person #1. He applied to grad school with all the qualifications needed to start the school year strong; he could always see over the fence.

I, on the other hand, could not.

I was only qualified and able to see over that fence *if* I

worked incredibly hard all summer to learn what I needed. Those months were my rock of equity, and to this day, I am incredibly grateful for it.

It was this ability to see over the fence that afforded me the opportunity to attend graduate school. This further education allowed me to have a career which enabled me to make an impact on a global scale—an impact that has created a ripple effect of change. This was all because I was given that rock, the act of equity I needed in order to begin.

THE RIPPLE EFFECT OF CHANGE

To this day, I clearly remember my interview for an internship at General Foods because it illustrates this powerful ripple effect of change. I remember when their Leader of Organizational Development asked me, *"Do you think leaders are born or can they be developed?"*

My answer: Strong leaders can be developed.
This answer has remained the same for me after all these years because I've seen it happen again and again and again.

When people are given the acts of equity that they need to thrive, the change they're able to make in their organizations, in themselves, and in the lives of those around them is nothing short of incredible.

When I see someone who starts to truly elevate their voice and understand the inherent power they have within themselves, I see their level of confidence build. With that newfound confidence, they branch out into various roles in their community and in their organizations. They develop themselves, they *invest* in themselves.

The ripple effect means that their careers start to expand because they have this new level of confidence now that they can see clearly to the other side. They always had the intelligence; that was never the issue. It was the confidence and the empowerment to be able to claim their spot at the table and speak up that was missing.

You see them taking on more significant opportunities, presenting at staff meetings, and leading their communities. Doors begin to open up for them, and all of a sudden—though it doesn't really happen that suddenly at all—you see them in leadership roles.

That's why I believe strong leaders are developed.

I've witnessed this over and over and over again in people from all walks of life. I've seen people go from being unsure and unwilling to contributing their best ideas and becoming strong leaders of value. It's beautiful.

It's this incredible ripple effect that happens when everyone can see over the fence.

CHAPTER TWO

HOW DO WE COMBAT THE "EQUITY IS PREFERENTIAL TREATMENT" MISUNDERSTANDING?

EQUITY AND PREFERENTIAL TREATMENT

We have already touched on the common misunderstanding that equity means giving preferential treatment to certain individuals and have used the equity analogy to provide a visual and clear-cut illustration as to why it hinders us all from being able to see over the fence.

It's this "equity as preferential treatment" misunderstanding I want to explore further. I believe it is the number one misconception holding us back from positive change in present-day society.

Remember, the ultimate goal is to tear down the fence entirely, so that everyone can see the beauty beyond. But taking down that fence is the harder, longer work. In order to do that work, in order to do more than just give rocks of equity, we must first *all* understand that equity is not a dirty word, nor is it giving preferential treatment.

The events of the 2020s in the United States and around the world offer a powerful case study in how equity has been misinterpreted as preferential treatment time and time again across many cultures. These events show us the real-world implications when this misunderstanding prevails.

I would like to begin by touching upon the anti-DEI (Diversity, Equity, and Inclusion) rhetoric that is sweeping present-day America. We didn't get here by happenstance. It is my hypothesis that in 2020, we saw the pendulum swing globally after the murder of George Floyd, a Black American man who was killed in Minnesota on May 25, 2020, by a white police officer who knelt on Floyd's neck for nine minutes.

During this time, people were shuttered at home amidst a global pandemic, and the only link to the outside world was through our televisions, computers, laptops, and phones. Our information and stories were coming to us solely through these mediums since we couldn't meet face-to-face and gather with our community.

We all watched in horror for those nine long minutes as Floyd pleaded for help and called out for his mother. Regardless of one's identity, we had nothing to do but watch and reflect on what was broken in our society—to witness such an event and ask what inequities and injustices got us here.

This opened the collective conversation to the plight of the African American in the present-day United States, and then, since online reaches have no bounds, we watched the conversation expand to all marginalized groups across countries globally. Solidarity was born from these online conversations around the globe.

There were calls for something to be done about the racial injustices that run rampant throughout our societies. There were protests in the streets—U.S.A., Germany, Turkey, China, Brazil, Canada—it didn't matter, we were all marching.

These events triggered the pendulum to swing towards social activism, and many rocks of equity got put in place because of it. People began to understand and question the inequities that existed within their own societies. The resulting calls to action sparked by the events of 2020 had some positive impact.

Disadvantaged groups were given more rocks of equity than ever before in the form of an increase in leadership programs for marginalized groups, programs to support women or minority-owned small businesses, an increase in conferences around diversity and inclusion, etc. A few specific examples of where these rocks of equity were being put in place include—

Equitable policy changes in our workplaces:

- Some companies set aspirational hiring goals to diversify leadership and staff. This was designed to increase representation of Black and other marginalized employees in order to better reflect real-world demographics.

- Internal audits were conducted to uncover the systemic biases that led to unfair pay and hiring policies. These audits reviewed promotion rates, pay gaps, and hiring practices to correct inequities that had existed for decades.

Equitable policy changes in our governments:

- In the United States, President Biden signed Executive Order 13985, titled *Advancing Racial Equity and Support for Underserved Communities Through the Federal Government.*[3] This order required federal agencies to assess their internal programs and evaluate whether they truly served all communities.
- The European Union's COST (European Cooperation in Science and Technology) research and innovation network funded a five-year study across 27 countries on identity check practices.[4] The study highlighted the disproportionate targeting of individuals based on ethnoracial appearance. Changes like training officers on implicit biases and establishing clearer guidelines were made.

These are just a sliver of the equitable commitments put into place in the early 2020s. From these examples, you can see that those in marginalized groups were being given the visibility and voice they'd previously lacked within our workplaces and governments.

These changes sparked hope. Finally, there was equitable progress, and it felt like soon those in the minority would be able to see over the fence, just like their majority peers.

THE PENDULUM SWINGS

As so often happens with change, it can start to breed discomfort—and so the pendulum begins to swing back the other way. This is what the world more recently witnessed. It is my opinion that somewhere around 2023, we started to see a rise in anti-Diversity, Equity, and Inclusion rhetoric, leaning into the idea of equity as preferential treatment.

This negative rhetoric began to gain traction and then made waves across social media as a response to the pendulum swinging toward building more equitable practices.

When I say equitable practices, I am referring to systems and policies that promote access, opportunity, and fair treatment for all. These practices do this with the goal that treatment is free from bias or favoritism by addressing the various barriers that an individual might face due to their unique circumstances.

As equitable practices increased with fervor, so too did negative and anti-DEI rhetoric. Why? Because as more equitable rocks were put in place, the majority (representing Person #1 in our equity analogy) perceived these acts of equity as "preferential treatment."

In this first image, it is assumed that everyone benefits from the same support. They are being treated **equally**.

Individuals are given different support to make it possible for them to have equal access to the view. They are being treated **equitably**.

All three can see the view without any support because the cause of inequality was addressed. The systemic barrier has been **removed**.

The misunderstanding was born from a mistaken perception that those in the majority would have their own rock taken away and lose their ability to see over the fence. When in reality, equity does not strip the opportunity to see over the fence from those who have always been able to. It simply levels the playing field so both minority and majority peers can see as well.

Because of this misunderstanding, feelings of equity as preferential treatment only grew post-pandemic when people began to return to in-person workplaces. Once we were all in the same physical place again, these changes, born from acts of equity, became more visible.

Meaning, you could now walk into the office and see with your very own eyes the Black woman who you perceived to get the promotion over you, when before she might not have been seriously considered. Or, your disabled coworker who might have been given a more flexible hybrid-work schedule when you were required to return to work in person five days a week.

These are just a few of the equitable policy changes that bred the sentiment of "unfairness" for some of those in the majority who were used to getting certain advantages. What they perceived as preferential treatment, were simply new practices put into place by their workplaces and communities to set their minority peers on more equal footing.

These equitable practices included pay transparency and equity adjustments, diversity in leadership, flexible work arrangements, cultural and religious accommodations, and inclusive hiring practices, to name a few. Yes, the playing field had changed. But I believe we made a critical error when those of us in leadership positions failed to do the work to explain *why*.

We assumed that because of the global outcry for change, everyone understood why this work needed to be done and why these equitable practices needed to be put into place, now more than ever. We assumed that those in the majority understood that the fence existed, when in reality, this isn't always the case because they have always been able to see what lies beyond it.

Because of this assumption, the misunderstanding of equity as preferential treatment grew and grew right under our noses and is currently manifesting itself in strict anti-Diversity, Equity, and Inclusion rhetoric from the U.S. government and a stripping back of Diversity, Equity, and Inclusion policies in both government agencies and certain private companies.

That is why the conversation we're having in this book is so important and extremely timely. For progress and change to stick, for us to debunk equity as a dirty word, and the misperception of it as preferential treatment, once and for all, we need to have an open dialogue. More importantly, we need to do equity right.

INCLUDING EVERYONE IN THE CONVERSATION

When I say doing equity right, I mean that we do not leave <u>anyone</u> behind. That includes those in the minority and those in the majority. This means that we need our majority allies to understand that they are part of the conversation, that they are not losing out on opportunities or their ability to see over the fence, even when rocks of equity are given to their peers in marginalized groups.

When building out equitable policies and practices, there is a key factor that is often missed and which creates this dissonance. It is one that needs to change because it only fuels the sentiment and perception of "preferential treatment," thus making it harder for our majority allies to come along with us.

This key factor is leaving a group of people out of the conversation. Let me explain.

Yes, the rise in rhetoric opposing Diversity, Equity, and Inclusion may have been born from what I like to call keyboard courage, with the bad actors' voices being elevated and broadcast widely by our social media algorithms. Making loud, angry statements and claims that very few others actually believe and that you would never wish to say to anyone's face, but that populate our screens constantly and influence opinions nonetheless.

But why have these voices of a few been given such weight? My answer: on some level, we failed to open the conversation and failed to do the hard work.

What do I mean by this? We had a group of people who, for all their lives, had lived with certain advantages that came from being in the majority. Advantages that they perceived were being taken away now that a focus was being placed on equitable changes.

This group of people now felt left out. They perceived that they were missing out on opportunities that used to be inherently theirs as more and more rocks of equity were put into place for their marginalized peers—rocks that worked to level the playing field.

It was not a mystery that they felt this way; their feelings about these changes were splashed all across our social media feeds. But because those of us making equitable change also knew that we were doing good work to ensure minority voices were finally being heard, some of us missed out on a key opportunity to do equity right. Let me explain.

Coming into the 2020 timeframe, a lot of emphasis on people of marginalized groups became the focal point of the conversation. These were folks who have been playing at a disadvantage their whole lives, whether because of race, ethnicity, gender, sexual orientation, or religion. Included is the group of people often referred to as the one-percenters who, from a classism standpoint, are predominantly white, male, and financially wealthy.

Then you have a third group. This group looked at what was happening and said to themselves, *Okay, well, I'm not rich, I don't identify with that socioeconomic status. I don't identify with anything other than being white. I am struggling to make ends meet, just like a lot of my minority peers. Where am I in this conversation?*

Some of us doing this work didn't explain the fence. We didn't include them in the dialogue about what the rocks of equity meant and why it felt like nothing extra was being given to them. We also didn't explain that nothing was being taken away. All that changed was putting in place the practices that allow all groups, including them, to begin at the same starting line so everyone has the ability to see over the fence.

Instead, this third group felt like they had been left out of the various social activism movements that have taken place in recent history, and they wondered where their voice was in the conversation. Which, of course, only added fuel to the fire of equity being misunderstood as preferential treatment.

This is one of the crucial areas where I believe those of us in leadership positions and on boards of social and institutional change may have missed the mark when it comes to equity. And why we—leaders, employers, employees, and community members—now need to have a clear and open conversation on how to do equity *right*, so that all voices are heard from every group. This is the only way to banish the "preferential treatment" myth and to instill with overwhelming clarity that equity has the power to level the playing field for *all*.

THE HARD WORK OF EQUITY

What happened in the early 2020s is not new, but it does show us clearly the repercussions of leaving anyone out of the conversation. Throughout history, certain groups have always been left out, such as:

- Indigenous peoples in Australia, who were excluded from the constitution and not counted in the national census until 1967.
- Dalits in India, who were systematically excluded from the public discourse under the country's caste system.
- Women, who were denied the right to vote in the United States until 1920, Switzerland until 1971, Ku-

wait until 2005, and Saudi Arabia until 2015 (just to name a few).

Like I said, what happened in the early 2020s is not new. But it is one of the gaps in how we've presented equity and has kept us from the progress and change that is possible when we all come together on equal footing.

In each individual country, there has always been a group/groups that have felt left behind, that have felt marginalized, and that didn't share the advantages that those in the majority had. But equity doesn't limit itself to race, gender, and different identities, and when done right, should be focused on the benefit for *all*. These benefits, I will dive deeper into in Part II of this book.

I believe that if we are truly doing the work to create an ecosystem of equality and inclusion, we don't leave anyone out. When the rocks of equity get put in place to uplift one group, we also ensure that other groups are brought in on the conversation as to *why* these changes are happening and how they are beneficial in the long run to both those in the minority and those in the majority.

This awareness—to leave no group feeling excluded— is key and what needs to change in the equity conversation. It's the missing piece that, when we fail to put in place, only perpetuates the misunderstanding that equity is synonymous with preferential treatment. I believe this is what added fuel to the fire in 2020s America, and why the pendulum of change has swung back forcefully the other way in the anti-Diversity, Equity, and Inclusion rhetoric, resulting in recent calls to banish equity from our terminology altogether.

There are calls for Diversity, Equity, and Inclusion staff to be put on immediate leave; documents on DEI are to be removed from government agency websites; employees are required to remove their preferred pronouns from their email signatures; and the State Department is to remove the link for its Office of Diversity and Inclusion from its website—some of these rapid changes.5

The question now is, how do we do equity right, so that everyone understands it is not a dirty word, and it is not preferential treatment, but it is simply leveling the playing field so we can all move within a fair and just world?

We will expand upon this further in upcoming chapters, but the short and sweet of it is this: In order to change the conversation around equity, we must do the harder work to ensure we are not leaving anyone behind. To do this, we must do three things:

1. Find out what it is that <u>everyone</u> needs to be able to succeed, and then offer the necessary opportunities to be able to put that into practice.
2. Look honestly at the systems, institutions, policies, and programs that are supposed to be for all people and ask, <u>are they truly for all?</u>
3. Acknowledge how different our individual paths are in life to open a dialogue so that we do not continue to misunderstand each other and can instead find <u>common ground.</u>

Going back to our rocks and fence analogy, the ultimate goal of equity is to get to a place where the fences are torn down. Then the rocks are no longer needed because we all move through the world on an equal playing field.

Sometimes, we do too much work putting the rocks in place without simultaneously doing the more long-term work of tearing down the fence (the systemic, institutional issues and isms that exist). This is the harder work.

Part of doing this harder work means not abandoning the person who's still standing on one rock while we give rocks of equity to our marginalized peers. It means not falling prey to the assumption that Person #1 in the equity illustration automatically understands he will still be able to see over the fence when change takes place. It is not functioning on the assumption that Person #1 understands the fence is even there in the first place.

It can be easy to highlight our differences and lean into our biases, convincing ourselves we cannot find common ground with people who feel that something is being taken from them. Instead, we must come out from behind our keyboards, devices, and algorithms designed to divide. We must come together face-to-face and have honest discussions through an open dialogue.

People are more likely to listen during these face-to-face conversations and may understand that sometimes life choices happen because of the barriers the fence provides. Minds can change, common ground can be found, and we can all band together to tear those fences down.

We just have to remember to listen *while* doing the work. Because if we don't understand the different viewpoints of the varied individuals that coexist with us in this wide world, how can we hope to create something for all, something that includes every group, race, gender, religion, and all other identities? We must include everyone in the conversation.

CHAPTER THREE

THE BARRIERS TO CHANGE—WHY IS UNDERSTANDING EQUITY SO HARD?

I t is my hope that you now have a clearer picture of why equity is not synonymous with preferential treatment, and also why it is so easily misunderstood. Together, we need to take this conversation one step further to paint a fuller picture of why understanding equity is so hard.

This exploration is not only to give you a strong foundation of understanding the word equity when reading the rest of this book, but so that when you engage in open conversation with your peers, you have the language necessary to explain the equity disconnect and pass the correct knowledge along.

In order to move our world further toward the goal of tearing down the fence—the systemic issues and isms—I believe we all have the responsibility to help our peers bridge the equity gap. This is the gap between seeing equity as a dirty word on one end of the chasm, to truly understanding why equity needs to be done for the benefit of all, on the other end. I am not naive to knowing that not everyone will embrace this conversation and dialogue. I also know that many marginalized groups do not feel it's their responsibility to educate others. But at some point, to open up the dialogue, we have to come together.

In this sentiment, the question to unpack now is: Why is understanding equity so hard? Why do misunderstandings continue to surround not only the word itself, but equity in practice?

I believe there are three main obstacles or barriers between where we stand now and the true change that can be made when equity is fully understood and embraced by our societies, our institutions, and our people.

These three obstacles are:

1. The end goal—equality—is the same, using different language to describe how we get there creates confusion.
2. The myth that equality equals fairness.
3. Lack of exposure to systemic issues.

Throughout this chapter, I'll guide you through each obstacle, and together we'll explore the historic misconceptions at the root of each one. We'll then clear them up, so that you can step into Part II of this book with clarity.

OBSTACLE #1: THE LANGUAGE BARRIER—HOW THE WORDS KEEP CHANGING

Equity has always existed, but over time, we've called it many different things due to political and social pressures.

Because the language around "equity" continues to change, it creates a barrier in understanding what the word truly means.

It's no wonder many of us are unclear or unsure of what equity is and how it differs from equality, a word that has not changed forms or meaning in the same way.

Let's use the vernacular in the United States as our example here.

Historically, we can see this change in language beginning with Affirmative Action, a concept first appearing in Executive Order 10925 issued by President Kennedy in 1961.6 Executive Order 10925's provisions were later expanded and incorporated in 1965, when President Lyndon B. Johnson issued Executive Order 11246, which reinforced and expanded upon the affirmative action principles set by Kennedy's order, particularly in federal contracting and employment.

Affirmative Action is a practice that seeks to correct the systemic inequalities that exist by increasing access. This access can come in the form of education, jobs, and other opportunities for those who have been historically disadvantaged (or even excluded) on the basis of race, religion, gender, or where they were born.

Affirmative action is equity in practice. It is a policy designed to bring fairness to the ways people are treated in education and workplaces, and aimed to ensure that this treatment is free from bias or favoritism. It was established to counteract systemic issues of discrimination both in workplace hiring and in education admissions, with a focus on women and Black Americans.

From the 1960s onwards, many used the terminology "affirmative action" more broadly to describe what they really meant—equity. But as time went on, affirmative action became increasingly politicized. The preferential treatment misunderstanding began to rear its ugly head here as well, with some calling it "reverse discrimination."

An example of this is the landmark 1978 case, Bakke v. Regents of the University of California, where the Supreme Court ruled that while affirmative action could be used in college admissions, strict racial quotas were unconstitutional. The Court ruled that race could be considered as one factor among others in admissions decisions, but that the University of California Davis School of Medicine's practice of reserving 16 out of 100 seats for minority students was unconstitutional.

This ruling caused a shift in both policy and public language around it. Why?

1. It associated Affirmative Action with Legal Risk.
2. It forced reframing of race-conscious policies.
3. It signaled a shift from repairing past actions to benefiting all through diverse learning environments.

In other words, the repercussions from the ruling signaled a shift away from affirmative action and towards diversity in order to avoid the risk that was now associated with the former—risk of equitable policies being labeled as "unconstitutional." With legal challenges and political pushback continuing, the language around affirmative action continued to change.

The focus away from Affirmative Action and towards diversity, expanded beyond race and gender to include LGBTQ+ identity, and the language was adapted to soften the political pushback. Affirmative action became "diversity initiatives" in the 2000s, and then Diversity, Equity, and Inclusion (DEI) gained prominence in the 2010s. Equity was explicitly added during this timeframe to address the fact that we do not all begin at the same place. It became clear that achieving true inclusion wasn't just about having diverse representation but also about addressing systemic barriers that prevent equal opportunity.

This language change to equity was most strongly felt in corporations and universities with procedures tied to hiring and admissions, directly speaking to Diversity, Equity, and Inclusion. These new initiatives were also where the common language started to actually incorporate the word equity into our public vernacular.

We know from Chapter Two that the backlash against the word "equity" resurfaced in the early 2020s. It begs us to ask the question: What happened between the early 2000s, when universities and corporations began including equity in their discourse, to when the very same word began to be misinterpreted and began to meet strong resistance.

It is my opinion that the sentiment of equity as a "dirty word" grew and grew because, just as affirmative action was misinterpreted in the 1970s and 1980s, equity, too, was equated with the same misunderstanding—giving people preferential treatment.

The events and changes by the new administration following the 2024 presidential election in the United States swiftly sparked outcry against the word equity itself. After just over a decade of consistent public use, the word is now under fire.

In 2025, new directives were issued that mandated the removal of specific terms from both public-facing institutional websites and educational materials. These changes extended across a wide range of organizations, including major universities, as well as nonprofits and other publicly funded entities. Further, the guidance stipulated that the presence of these flagged terms in grant proposals would result in automatic scrutiny, effectively disqualifying the application from serious consideration.

Among the terms targeted for removal: equity, equitable, and equitableness.

As a result of this guidance, private organizations, federal contractors, individuals, and nonprofit organizations who need access to government grants for funding have begun removing these "trigger words" from their grant applications and public-facing websites. In order to follow the new guidance, the word equity, like its counterparts, like Affirmative Action before it, is being stripped away.

Just as happened with the changing language in the past, public-facing organizations and institutions are now looking to replace equity with something similar to equity (all but synonymous) so that they may continue the necessary work of equity without the backlash—and the risk of being flagged.

What word are they using instead? *Fairness.* A term that has a strong relationship with equity, and one that we will be delving into in greater detail below.

Regardless of the language around it changing, equity is what is needed in this moment—equity in action. And it is our responsibility to educate ourselves and banish the misconceptions and obstacles, so that we all can benefit from the power of equity in action.

OBSTACLE #2: THE MYTH OF EQUALITY VS. FAIRNESS

Let's dive into fairness.

Many people were taught that equality means treating everyone fairly. But equality and fairness are not one and the same. Let's break down both words to help us better understand how and why they're different.

Equality means that everyone—regardless of age, gender, sexual orientation, or ethnic background—receives the same resources and opportunities.

Equality = treating everyone the same regardless of individual differences or circumstances.

Fairness means doing what's right to ensure everyone has equal access, based on the context of the situation. Access is the key differentiator here. Since we're all starting from different places, access for one person may be different for someone else.

Fairness = giving people what they need to succeed, even if that means treating people differently in order to reach a just outcome.

For a visual analogy, the difference between equality, equity, and fairness would look a little like this:

- **Equality** is giving everyone the same size box to stand on in order to see over a fence.
- **Equity** is giving taller people smaller boxes, and shorter people taller boxes, so that everyone can see over the fence.
- **Fairness** considers whether it's just that there's a fence there in the first place.

We will dive deeper into equity's role here in detail in future chapters. For now, to help us banish this particular obstacle (the myth of equality vs. fairness), I'd like to break down equality and fairness even further by giving an actionable example.

Picture three children sitting on the curb outside a candy store.

Child #1 has a quarter.

Child #2 has a dime.

Child #3 has no money.

All three children want this delicious candy bar that costs 50 cents. All things being equal, I give each child a quarter. I've given them all an equal amount of money, assuming they will all now be able to purchase the candy bar.

But this isn't the case.

Instead, only Child #1, who already had a quarter in the first place, now has the 50 cents needed to buy the candy bar. The other two children have 35 cents and 25 cents, respectively. They are left hungry and do not have the *access* (or resources) needed to purchase the candy bar.

This example shows us where equality falls short of fairness.

If we look at this example again, this time through the lens of fairness, you will see something different. If I'm being fair, I want to make sure that each child has access to the candy bar. So I give Child #1, who has a quarter, 25 cents. I give Child #2, who has a dime, 40 cents. Lastly, I give Child #3 who has nothing, 50 cents. Now, all three children have the 50 cents—the access needed—to purchase and enjoy their very own candy bar. Giving each child the money they needed to buy the candy bar, in this example, were the acts of equity. These acts of equity enabled fairness and everyone was able to have access to the candy bar.

Notice how the resources each child required to succeed at this task were different based on how much money they had to begin with. In this example, the money is representative of the varied and individual circumstances we all begin with. Because we do not start with the same opportunities and resources, the access we need to succeed also varies.

This candy bar example demonstrates the impact of placing too much focus on equality in an unfair world. Because equality does not account for our individual circumstances, it falls short in practice. Instead, it is *fairness* that ensures we all have access to the opportunities we require to see over the fence or to buy the candy bar.

That is why equity is so necessary. Because it puts actions in place to achieve fairness, where equality does not.

To call back upon our definition of equity in Chapter One, we can now add another layer to our understanding of equity based on the candy bar example.

> **Equity** is defined as being just and fair in the way that people are treated. This treatment, while free from bias or favoritism, tailors support to individual needs so that everyone can have access to the opportunities they need to thrive.
>
> *Equity = actions done to tailor support to individual needs, which enables fairness.*

In the simplest terms, equity is needed because it puts actions in place to achieve fairness. It acknowledges our varied starting points and aims to level the playing field. Not so one person can get ahead at the expense of another, but so that we all have equal *access* (the 50 cents needed to buy the candy bar).

You can see that equity is not a dirty word. It is not terminology we should strike from our vocabularies. Instead of leaning into pressures to change the meaning of the word yet again, we should be turning up the conversation around equity. We should be speaking more openly about it than ever before, and educating our peers in order to banish the confusion around the word, so that we can make bolder strides towards fairness and access.

Equality doesn't consider fairness, equity *does*. This is why in practice and in real-world circumstances, our rhetoric and action must focus on equity first, so that we may all get to taste the sweetness of that candy bar.

OBSTACLE #3: LACK OF EXPOSURE TO SYSTEMIC ISSUES

The third obstacle people often face in understanding equity comes from a lack of exposure to systemic issues. What I mean by this is that when people don't experience systemic oppression firsthand, they have a tendency to assume the issues don't exist.

When I say systemic issues, I am referring to problems that are prevalent because they are built into the structure, culture, or rules of a system. These issues exist within societies, in workplaces, in public and private institutions, in cultural groups, etc.

Returning to our rock and fence analogy, because Person #1 has always been able to see over the fence (so never comes up against the systemic issues his peers face as an ongoing barrier), it is common for that person to not even realize the fence exists in the first place. He doesn't look down or around to notice that some visible (or invisible) barrier stands in the way of his peers being able to see over it.

An example of a systemic issue is the gender pay gap, where worldwide, women earn less for every dollar earned by men for the same work. For decades there have been missing guardrails on fairness of salaries, equal access to employment opportunities, and implicit gender biases that continue to prevail today. To highlight an example of the global gender pay gap, let's look at the statistics reported by Equal Pay Today, a Los Angeles based organization dedicated to closing the gender and racial pay gap by providing transparency around the facts and numbers:[7]

United States: On average, women earn 83.6% of what men earn.

Australia: On average, women earn 83% of what men earn.

European Union: The gender pay gap ranges by country, with women earning 95%-83% of what men earn.

India: On average, women earn 75.19% of what men earn.

In developing nations, this gender pay gap sees an even steeper divide because of other systemic issues that exist, such as limited access to education and employment opportunities for women.

What's more, these statistics from Equal Pay Today tell us that at the current rate of progress, we won't see this gender pay gap close for 134 years. This expected rate of change is jarring and promptly expresses why we need the work of equity now more than ever.

Bringing it back to Obstacle #3—a lack of exposure to systemic issues—let's now frame this obstacle through the lens of the gender pay gap. Maria and James were both hired at the same company, both with similar qualifications and a shared passion for their work. But from the moment they joined, the system they entered was already tilted in ways they didn't fully realize.

Maria, though just as skilled and dedicated as James, was offered a starting salary that was significantly lower than his. James took home more money from day one, which allowed him to take on personal projects, attend conferences, and invest in opportunities that broadened his horizons outside of work. Maria, on the other hand, felt the weight of financial strain, even as she put in the same effort, sometimes more, to make her mark.

Over time, the subtle yet persistent biases within the company began to show. James was promoted first—after all, the company's old thinking held that men were more likely to perform better, even when the numbers told a different story. Maria's quarterly evaluations consistently outshone James's, yet he moved ahead of Maria. He received a promotion that came with a 12% raise, further widening the gap between their salaries.

For Maria, the path to promotion wasn't as clear. The system still leaned on outdated assumptions about who was "leadership material". And though Maria proved herself again and again, she had to fight harder for recognition. It took her two additional years to be promoted to the next level.

Even then, her raise was only 10%—which is smaller than James's 12% salary increase. And because Maria started with a lower salary, that 10% raise didn't have the same impact on her financial advancement. By the time she was promoted, James had already moved up again, this time with another 12% increase in his salary.

Maria worked just as hard, if not harder, but the system seemed to reward James simply because of who he was. The gap between their salaries kept growing, not because of her lack of ability or dedication, but because of biases ingrained in how promotions and raises were determined. And every day, this pattern continued on and on. Not only for James and Maria, but for employees in workplaces around the world.

The gender pay gap represents only one systemic issue, but as you can see, there are real-world consequences to the way our systems have been set up. Because they were structured around the majority, they automatically provide more opportunities for those belonging to this group. And unfortunately in doing so, often leave out those who do not.

It is important to note that this, and other systemic issues, are not caused by one tangible thing or event. Instead, they happen over time, often having longstanding historical roots. More than that, they are typically very difficult to see. Why? They feel normal because they have "always been that way."

Does that phrase sound familiar?

At one time or another, we have all heard someone say, "Well, that's the way it's always been, so why do I have to change my behavior or opinions now?"

Whether that phrase comes from the mouth of those receiving the benefits by being a part of the majority or those in power, it is often said freely in our current society.

This represents the foundational problem of not seeing the systemic issue. Someone who has always had access to certain opportunities can easily assume that everyone else does too. It calls into question the "privilege debate," which is the tendency for some people who have benefited from the current systems to interpret discussions of systemic inequity as a personal attack.

Let's explain the privilege debate with a personal example. I remember standing among a group of white parents who were talking about their 16-year-old sons getting their learner's permit, and how each parent was teaching their son how to drive. The group turned to me and asked about how my son was coming along in learning to drive as he was about the same age.

I explained to them that my husband and I had to have "the talk" with our son as well as teaching him how to drive. The group didn't know what I meant by "the talk". So I went on to explain the need for Black parents to teach their sons what they need to do when they are pulled over by the police.

They looked at me with this incredulous look on their faces as if I was blaming them for having to have this discussion with our son to ensure he was able to survive an encounter with the police as a Black male. I was not indicting them, I was simply expressing how my reality was different from theirs as white parents.

But this was not their reality, and so something as simple as teaching your son to drive, certainly shouldn't be different for me than it was for them. But it is. Just because they don't need to educate their sons on how to handle an encounter with police, doesn't mean it's not both a reality and a barrier that Black parents and their sons deal with on a daily basis. This is a clear example of the privilege debate. In this case, we don't mean financial privilege, but the privilege to move throughout the world without a barrier that your diverse peers face on a daily basis.

The change that's been called for—whether that be in 2020 during the protests over the George Floyd murder, when Apartheid ended in South Africa in 1990, or even as far back as 1865 when slavery was abolished in the United States—change causes friction.

It can be more comforting to continue in old thought patterns, to think, "I just want it to be like it was, back when it was easy." But you have to consider privilege.

I remember years ago being in a meeting and the leader started talking about how he longed for the "good old days", and I looked to a colleague who was disabled. She and I had shared stories privately about how we were bullied in school for what we looked like because we looked different than others—me as a Black woman, and her as a disabled woman. The look in her eyes during that meeting mirrored the look she saw in mine. We did not "long for the good old days" because they weren't good for us in many ways. They weren't easier, they were harder. We faced numerous barriers because of our physical appearance alone.

I would suggest two counterarguments to the "good old days" philosophy here:

1. It is "easy" because those who long for the good old days are not the ones facing the systemic issues that are holding others back. Longing for the good old days when others are avidly calling for change, begs

them to look around and ask, "Is there a fence, a barrier, that I cannot see?"

2. The world is ever-evolving. For some, when they've been in a position of power for their entire lives, there can be a very real fear of losing that power. When there is a threat to losing a certain level of privilege for the sake of a more even playing field, it creates a lack of understanding of why their world is changing.

We cannot discount how true these two things are— or how valid the resistance and fear around change can be. This is why we spoke at length in Chapter Two about bringing everyone, especially those who have always been in the majority, into the conversation.

For many of our marginalized peers, there is and has always been a very real barrier holding them back. They cannot hope to see it changed without support from majority allies who understand the repercussions of systemic issues and the necessity for rocks of equity to be put in place. Not to strip anything away from the majority, but to level the playing field for their minority peers. This is why banishing this obstacle of misunderstanding is so important, and why I am writing this book—to foster this education and understanding for all.

Giving rocks of equity to level the playing field while doing the harder work of tearing down the fence are necessary to slowly bring about change to the structure and systems that got us here. We must also acknowledge that it's going to take a long time to bring that level of true change.

Referring back to the gender pay gap statistic as an example, it is predicted that it will take over 130 years to close the gender pay disparity worldwide because of the systemic issues that have been in place for far longer. This is the timeline of the harder work.

This is also why we speak about equity in policy and in practice as smaller rocks aimed at leveling the playing field, in addition to smashing down the fence. For example, putting in place employee resource groups to address the issues faced by women in organizations is an example of a "rock" of equity.

Forming a women's resource group in the workplace can help women employees with both personal and professional needs. It can also help male allies become better leaders, to understand the unique challenges women face, and to better meet the needs of all employees. Finally, resource groups encourage the organization to build a culture of inclusion, which is attractive to current employees (increases retention and decreases turnover), and is attractive to future candidates who are in the job market looking for organizations to join.

Because smaller rocks of equity lift everyone to see over the fence, that is the change we can make now. Dismantling the systemic issues that exist within our societies will take much, much longer.

I want to acknowledge that on some level, it is normal for it to feel easier to go on as it's always been, instead of confronting the big changes that need to happen to tear down the fence. If you've ever felt that way, please do not let it discourage you from being a part of the necessary work of equity.

If we do not take a serious look around us, it can be easy to miss the systemic reasons why people are struggling. Whether or not you've faced certain systemic issues yourself, it is well within your power to look around and notice, perhaps for the first time, the barriers and fences that are in place.

It is time that we all really look, and collectively acknowledge, the need for change.

CHAPTER FOUR

WHY DO WE NEED EQUITY NOW MORE THAN EVER?

OUR WORLD HAS CHANGED, SO MUST WE

For the purposes of this book, and to clearly explain the need for equity and the barriers to change that prevent an equal playing field, I will continue to use the terms "majority" and "minority" as we currently know them. But we will spend this chapter exploring why the terms majority and minority only become more and more outdated as our demographics (characteristics of our population such as gender and race) continue to change in the modern world.

It is important to note here that I do not suggest we lump everyone who is a person of color into one homogeneous "minority" group. We are all different, individually and culturally, and should be celebrated as such. I also do not support an "us" versus "them" narrative, pitting one group of people against another.

I do, however, support equity, which champions a level playing field for all, so that each and every one of us can have equal access to opportunities both personally and professionally.

The varied systemic issues that exist across cultures, countries, and continents did not happen overnight, and they were not built by happenstance. We didn't get where we are today in a short period of time, and we can't expect all of the systemic issues and biases to right themselves overnight.

In order to change these deeply ingrained systemic issues, we will first need to look at our actual systems—the interconnected structures within our society—including those that exist within our institutions, housing, education, and global corporations. It's going to take decades to look at all of these systems, but that is the work that needs to be done. I believe we have to get granular and look at the inequities that exist, and then establish new systems that reflect our current world.

Many longstanding systemic issues were built and created, yes. But they were built and created in a different world. I can recall when I was a child of about 10 years old, my father was leaving our house one evening after dinner and heading out the door. I asked him where he was going and he said he was going to vote.

Young as I was, I did know that a presidential election was occurring, and I remember seeing the news and hearing that the Democratic candidate was way behind the Republican candidate in the polls and was projected to lose. I asked my father who he was going to vote for, and he said he was going to vote for the Democratic candidate. I asked him why, when it was obvious that he was going to lose.

He said that when he was born, people who looked like us weren't allowed to vote. He'd watched his father, my grandfather, be turned away from the voting booth time and time again just for being a Black man. Through my eyes as a child, I couldn't understand why the laws would prohibit a person from voting because of the color of their skin, but that was the system that voting had been built within. My father said that as long as he was alive, he would always exercise his right to vote, no matter who he voted for, because it was something that people like his father and other brave men and women had fought for, and in some cases, had died for.

Just one generation of Black Americans before me, remembers the feeling of being turned away from the voting booth, for nothing more than the color of their skin. Maybe you too know someone who was turned away. Today, it is a given that voting in the United States is not determined by the color of your skin. People fought for a system to be changed that had once held them back. Change is not a bad thing, and it is inevitable. I believe it's the work we do amidst the challenge that ensures the change is for the better—change that reflects our current world and all of the people in it.

This is the reason we cannot let shifting language around equity or fear of a new status quo, as discussed in the last chapter, stop us from the change that is coming or the change that is already here. It is also why we must be brave enough to take a long, hard look at what is not working to build new systems that work in the world as it exists today.

During the period of time when many of our current systems were built:

- Slavery was legal in the United States and numerous other European countries for hundreds of years.
- Women didn't have rights—whether that be the right to vote, to open a bank account, own property, or the right to divorce or leave an abusive marriage.

LGBTQ+ people didn't have the right to marry, adopt children, serve openly in the military, or the right to legal protection from discrimination.

Globally, we have seen changes in all of the above circumstances, although in certain countries, women and LGBTQ+ people still lack the same rights as those in the majority. With that said, on a global scale, our world today is vastly different from the conditions of hundreds of years prior.

Yet many of the systems and structures that were established during these times still stand today. It's no wonder systemic issues such as the gender pay gap still exist, why racial biases still occur, and why discrimination against our LGBTQ+ peers is still so prevalent. The world changed, but the systems that support our daily life have not changed at the same rate.

Yes, we have seen rights given to the groups I noted in the examples listed above, as well as many others. But the hard work of equity is still needed until we actually tear down the fences and dismantle systemic issues that continue to hold minority groups back within systems that were not built for them.

One example of an outdated policy—a system that has not adapted at the same rate as our daily life and continues to hold one or more groups back—is the retirement age requirement in many countries. Traditionally set around 65 years old, these policies fail to account for increasing life expectancy and the shifting demographics of the workforce. With declining birth rates and a growing senior population, many economies are facing labor shortages, yet older adults who are willing and able to work are often forced into retirement due to rigid age-based policies.8

Another outdated policy is the lack of comprehensive care and support for aging at home. Despite the fact that 85% of older adults prefer to remain in their homes rather than institutional settings, many government programs still prioritize funding for nursing homes over home-based care.9 This fails to reflect the changing needs and preferences of an aging population.

Additionally, immigration policies in some countries remain restrictive despite the fact that net immigration is becoming a crucial factor in population growth. Without immigration, some nations would experience population decline, yet outdated immigration laws continue to limit the ability of skilled workers to relocate and contribute to economies in need of labor.10

These policies, and so many more, need modernization to align with the demographic realities of 2025 and to ensure economic sustainability. That is the work that is being done, but we need more support. We need more allies to stand for equity in a moment of change when the word equity is under threat.

SHIFTING DEMOGRAPHICS AND THE NEW RACIAL LANDSCAPE

One of the main reasons we cannot look away at this moment is the simple fact that the world has already changed. Women now have the right to vote in 198 countries and territories.[11] We've seen a global expansion of marriage equality with same-sex marriage legalized in 38 countries.[12] And countries like Germany and Iceland have passed national laws requiring companies to provide equal pay for equal work to combat the gender and racial pay gaps. These are just a few of the visible ways that our world has made shifts toward equity, and there have been countless changes globally—both big and small.

The impact of this equitable change remains the same. What was once acceptable is no longer such.

For example, slave trade was abolished in the British Empire in 1833, and although it took three more decades, slavery was later abolished in America in 1865. Now, almost 200 years later, it is not legal to own another human being <u>anywhere</u> in the world. Slavery used to be a reality of daily life, now it is unfathomable. Similarly, women were not allowed to vote or open a bank account without their husband, now this is daily reality and we wouldn't expect anything less.

These examples show us a starkly different world. Resisting this reality does not change the fact that it is true. It simply delays the progress that is coming and puts us at odds with one another, as some resist the concept of change, while others accept and embrace it.

As our world continues to become more and more interconnected, demographics are naturally shifting. The United States is witnessing one of the largest population shifts in the 2000s. William H. Frey, an internationally regarded demographer, published his book *Diversity Explosion: How New Racial Demographics Are Remaking America* in 2014. In it, he highlights the increasing racial diversity in the United States, terming it the "Browning of America".

Frey argues that this diversity boom will not lead to a more divided nation, as older generations fear. Instead, this profound racial change will foster a less-divided nation, actually combatting the declining economic and social growth, instead of being the cause of it.

A few ways Frey suggests these demographic shifts are beneficial to society as a whole:

- As the aging white population retires, younger, more diverse generations will infuse new vitality into the labor force, helping prevent economic stagnation.
- The rise in interracial marriages and multiracial identities, bring people together. This blending of cultures contributes to the breakdown of racial barriers and promotes social cohesion.
- Minorities are moving into suburban areas traditionally dominated by white populations at an increased rate. This leads to more integrated commu-

nities with daily interactions among diverse groups, fostering mutual understanding.

As you can see, these demographic shifts open the door for us to position diversity as a strength, bringing cohesion rather than division to our daily interactions.

Frey also refers to the "new minorities" experiencing significant population growth. These groups include Hispanics, Asians, and multiracial Americans. This population shift is reshaping preexisting demographics. Demographers highlight regional shifts, neighborhood segregation, and interracial marriage as just some of the contributors to this change. What does Frey say will be the ultimate outcome of these shifts?

No racial majority: No single ethnic or racial group holds the majority share of the population.13 Some of the advantages of this no racial majority can be seen in the example above, and we will dive deeper into the benefits of a diverse society in Part III of this book.

I'd like to now highlight a few (of many) statistics gathered from the U.S. Census and The Pew Research Center that reflect these changing demographics that signify we are well on our way to no racial majority in the United States.

- The U.S. Census Bureau projects that by the year 2045, white Americans are expected to make up less than 50% of the population.
- The new census projections indicate that, for youth under 18—the post-millennial population—minorities will outnumber whites by 2020,[14] meaning at the

time of writing, this is already the case. The Pew Research Center[15] takes this projection a step further with data indicating that by 2065, the U.S. will not have one single ethnic or racial majority.

Moreover, this phenomenon is not limited to the United States. Demographic changes are happening globally. For example, minority groups are projected to rise from 10% of the British population in 2006 to 40% by 2050. These trends suggest that white-British will no longer be the majority ethnic group in the U.K. by 2070.16

Why is equity pivotal in this moment of demographic change? I believe that demographic diversity without equity only leads to tension, not inclusion. Simply having a diverse population does not automatically create a world of fairness and unity. Instead, it is through intentional, equitable policies in our schools, workplaces, and government that make the difference, so that our systems better reflect the reality of our changing demographics.

Two things are important to note about these shifts before we move forward:

1. Younger generations are leading this demographic change, with higher birth rates among Hispanic, Black, Asian, and multiracial populations contributing to a more multicultural society as a whole.

2. When we speak about the "white majority," this is not wholly reflective of the world we live in. In fact, there are only select countries, including the United States and Britain, where the white population *is* the majority.

Let us dive deeper into this second point.

The definition of the **global majority** refers specifically to a collective term used to describe Indigenous, Asian, African, Latin American, or mixed-heritage populations. These people make up over 80% of the global population.

Although this is statistically true, in countries like the United States, the historic focus has been placed on the white majority, and many systems were set up and designed by and for the white majority. Historic systems such as legal segregation and Jim Crow laws ensured white access to the best schools, neighborhoods, and jobs. Also more recent systems show disparities such as in our criminal justice system, where Black and Latinos are disproportionately targeted by police and face harsher sentencing.

Likewise, several countries beyond the US have historically centered their systems around a white majority,[17] shaping institutions, policies, and societal structures to reflect and benefit the white demographic. Some notable examples include:

Canada – Many of its legal, political, and economic systems were historically designed around a white European settler majority, often marginalizing Indigenous peoples and non-European immigrants. The legacy of colonialism continues to influence policies today.

Australia – The country's early policies, such as the White Australia Policy (which restricted non-European immigration until the mid-20th century), were explicitly designed to maintain a white majority. Indigenous

Australians have faced systemic exclusion from governance and land rights for much of the country's history.

United Kingdom – While the U.K. has long been a diverse empire, its institutions—from government to education—were historically built around a white British majority. The legacy of colonial rule shaped policies that often prioritized white Britons over immigrants from former colonies.

South Africa – Under apartheid (1948 – 1994), the government explicitly structured laws and institutions to benefit the white minority, enforcing racial segregation and economic disparity. While apartheid ended, systemic inequalities have continued to persist.

New Zealand – Like Australia, New Zealand's early governance and legal systems were designed around a white settler majority, often marginalizing the Indigenous Māori population.

Argentina and Chile – While these countries have Indigenous populations, their national identities and institutions were historically shaped by European immigration, particularly from Spain and Italy, reinforcing a white-majority focus.

But if Black, Brown, Asian, Hispanic, and multiracial people make up the majority of the world's population, why do we continuously refer to these groups as "minorities" and why haven't our practices and policies naturally shifted along with changing demographics?

That has been called into question in recent years, with numerous organizations and even the U.K. government changing their use of terms like "BAME" (Black, Asian, and Minority Ethnic) to "ethnic minorities" and "people from ethnic minority backgrounds" to foster a sense of belonging and understanding for people who have felt less-than as a minority in the country that they live in—even when they represent the majority on a global scale.[18] The goal is for *everyone* to have the terminology to describe minority populations in a more inclusive manner representative of the fact that these groups, in fact, make up a majority of the world's population.

DIVERSITY OPENS THE DOOR TO INNOVATION

Let's look more at the concept of the global majority. Coined by Rosemary Campbell Stephens, a British educator and activist of African Caribbean descent and heritage. Her Global Majority Leadership Framework "decentres parasitic socially and politically constructed systems that, minoritise, negatively racialise, and routinely exclude people of the global majority through 'normalised' systems and processes."[19]

Put more simply, the global majority framework champions more equitable spaces, insisting that our varied and diverse backgrounds and our differences are strengths to effect positive change. Similar to William Frey's theory that the changing demographic landscape in the United States will lessen the majority/minority divide and create a less-divided nation, so too does Rosemary Campbell Stephens posit that it is our leading strength to have varied diverse communities—both ethnically diverse but also diversity consisting of *all* identities (persons with disabilities and other marginalized groups). When we all bring our unique and varied perspectives to the table, *that is how we innovate.* We will further discuss innovation in detail in Part III of this book.

This is precisely why I am calling for all of us to reframe the word equity, not get rid of it. Now more than ever, our world is craving a level playing field. Only when we all have the opportunity to see over the fence, can we truly build from a place where everyone has a seat at the table.

Unique perspectives are fostered when majority (historically white) and minority (Black, Hispanic, Asian, and multiracial, and other identities) peers are represented equally in positions of leadership, influence, and impact. This allows for multidimensional ideas and varied outlooks. This opens the doors to unparalleled innovation.

We will dive further into this in future chapters, but put simply, in order to capitalize on this positive potential for change, we must do more than just the surface or "performative" work.

Performative diversity and inclusion (D&I) efforts are actions that prioritize optics over meaningful change. One common example is when companies release public statements supporting diversity but fail to implement policies that address systemic inequalities within their organization.

For instance, after the murder of George Floyd in 2020, many corporations issued statements condemning racism and pledging commitment to diversity. However, some of these companies did not take concrete steps to improve hiring practices, address pay disparities, or create inclusive workplace cultures. What's more, employees often notice when D&I efforts are superficial—such as hosting diversity panels without addressing internal biases or by promoting a few diverse hires without actually changing workplace policies.[20]

Another example is when companies celebrate multicultural holidays or launch diversity-themed marketing campaigns but fail to support marginalized employees in meaningful ways. If a company promotes Black History Month or Pride Month externally but does not have equitable promotion opportunities or inclusive benefits for Black or LGBTQ+ employees, their efforts can be seen as performative.[21]

This is the surface work.

You have heard me say in the last chapter that we need to do the *hard work* of equity. Acts of equity (the rocks) like equitable promotion opportunities, inclusive workplace cultures, and improved hiring practices tear down the fence and support the systemic change that needs to happen. We have to do both to make lasting and sustainable change. Similarly, Stephens says we must go a step beyond just who is sitting at the table and look at "what is done there."

We all need to give the rocks of equity, the opportunities for everyone to see over the systemic barriers that have been holding them back, so that diverse peers may have a seat at the leadership table. But then we must take it a step further, and from that diverse table do the hard work of looking around at the systems that are no longer working. And change them.

When we do that, our leaders accurately represent and reflect the world that we live in. This change has a trickle-down effect not only to those in positions of power, but to every member of the community, so that everyone is afforded the opportunities they need to thrive personally and professionally. This is the exact work of equity, and why we need it more now than ever before.

BUILDING A BETTER WORLD

To recap, the demographics of our world have already changed and will continue to do so. In the United States, we are approaching a time where there will be no racial majority. As a result, the policies, structures, and systems that were built to provide more opportunities to majority populations need to be restructured to reflect these new population demographics.

That is how future generations can build more cohesive and innovative communities. And it is something that cannot wait.

It is time to do the hard work of equity. To look at our limiting systems and ask, *are they truly for everyone?* Where they are not, we must alter them. This is how we may support our youth as they enter the higher education system and when they enter the workforce. It is how we can bolster those in older generations who have worked relentlessly to build something more for themselves but have been repeatedly halted by the systemic barriers that are in place. No matter how they identify, it is time to give everyone a seat at the table.

The current demographic change necessitates the work of equity and begs us to seize this opportunity to not leave anyone behind as our majority and minority populations begin to look different. Just as Frey suggests in his own work, I too believe that this population shift will foster stronger societies. The how of this will be our predominant focus in Part III.

I believe that we have an opportunity to seize this moment of change to do better than we ever have before. Because, when done right, equity enhances social stability, increases innovation, and promotes economic growth. This is why we will place our focus on these three things in the next part of this book.

This positive change only comes when we commit to standing up and doing the work. The goal is that the systemic barriers that have prevented diverse people from equal opportunities for generations do not threaten to hold back larger and larger portions of the population as demographics continue to shift.

Please note that as these demographics continue towards Frey's defined "no racial majority," the white population is just as included here as our Black, Asian, Hispanic, Indigenous, and mixed peers.

Remember, the work of equity is not to leave <u>anyone</u> out of the conversation.

PART II

CHAPTER FIVE

WHY IS EQUITY NECESSARY IN A MERIT-BASED SYSTEM?

THE BEST PERSON FOR THE JOB

In recent years, many have talked about the need for an emphasis on "meritocracy" and less on the need or use of equity. It has been part of the discussion in both the private and the public sectors; it is discussed in the halls of academic universities, and among for-profit and non-profit leaders. From my forty years of experience in Human Resources and as a Diversity, Equity, and Inclusion Leader, I can speak to why I believe we need equity first—<u>before</u> we can hope to see a true meritocracy.

To explain, let's take a look at the concept of a meritocracy, and why equity is necessary in a merit-based system—whether that be in our workplaces, higher education institutions, non-profits, government, etc.

> **Meritocracy.** When I speak about a meritocracy, I mean hiring or selecting people according to merit alone. In other words, meritocracy assumes that anyone can achieve what they desire if they just work hard enough.
>
> *Meritocracy = Rewarding individuals based on how well they perform or what they contribute.*

We cannot have a true meritocracy <u>until</u> everyone has equal access to opportunities without barriers or obstacles standing in their way. If we hope to hire the "best" person for the job, purely based on merit alone, we all need to be standing on a level playing field. We currently do not.

This is why I believe that we all have a responsibility, now more than ever, to talk about what hasn't worked, and why, even in a merit-based system. We need the work of equity to bring about true progress—progress that makes a merit-based system possible.

Let's discuss.

A meritocracy is a great idea in theory, but it also assumes that everyone starts from the same place, has the same opportunities, the same education, and the same advantages. If you've read this far into the book, you know by now that this isn't the case. We all start from varied places with unequal access.

In the case of our candy bar example from Chapter Three, a meritocracy assumes that each of the three children would start the day with the same 50 cents in their back pocket, and each can automatically buy the candy bar if they desire it.

Similarly, within the workplace and hiring process, meritocracy says you always hire the "best" person for the job. Why? Because through the lens of meritocracy, we all have equal access to the 50 cents, and we can all buy the candy bar if we want it, so it's just about who works hard enough to get it.

Yes, in a perfect world (and in a true meritocracy), hiring the best person for the job would be the only qualification. We would be assessed based on our skills and capabilities alone, regardless of how we identify. We'd be solely judged by the content of our character and not the color of our skin, our gender, our identity, or our religion.

Sounds good, right?

But as we know, inherent and implicit biases around race, gender, sexuality, religious identity, and other identities are a fact of life in today's society. The systemic barriers that exist mean that the "best person for the job" may not even be on your radar because they have not had the equal access necessary to give them a seat at the leadership table in the first place. The "best person for the job" may be overlooked because of the biases that exist within our society and affect our hiring process. They may be overlooked because of things like not having the right clothes, or their hair doesn't look professional, or they don't speak in a language that we all understand.

THROWING UP THE CURTAIN

To more fully explain why a true meritocracy is not feasible from where we stand at the time of writing this book. Let's take a look at blind auditions in some of the top orchestras.

Data tells us that as late as 1970, the top five orchestras in the United States had fewer than 5% women out of about 100 musicians. That's less than five women.

Because of this large disparity, they wanted to expand diversity within individual orchestras to include more women to better reflect, and more accurately represent, the population of the cities where the orchestras were located. In order to do this, many orchestras began instituting "blind auditions" where bias is taken out by removing gender indicators at the first step of the interview process.

In this case, blind auditions meant that they had closed auditions where the person who was auditioning for a spot in the orchestra, whether they were male or female, played from behind a curtain so that the assessors could not see them.

Interestingly enough, blind auditions achieved what the orchestras had set out to do. The curtain took out the systemic and internal biases of how the interviewers perceived the musical capabilities of women versus men, and the judges had to select the candidates purely based on the quality of their play.

The process of blind auditions continued, and the needle began to move. Ten years after first implementing the new audition process, top orchestras crossed the mark of 10% female musicians, doubling their number of women orchestra members. By 1997, they averaged 25% women, and in the mid-2000s, some of the orchestras have reached 30% now .[22]

This demonstrates how the work of equity moves us towards a more even playing field. But it also highlights the number of years required to do the work that needs to be done to tear down the fence.

In just over thirty years, orchestras increased their percentage of women six times over because blind auditions took gender bias completely out of the equation. They were *truly* picking the person who was the best candidate for the job based on their musical skills and capabilities.

That's a meritocracy—picking the best people.

However, the fact that they had to put the curtain up in the first place is proof that a true meritocracy doesn't exist. We can't make the leap to restore a meritocracy until we first do the work of equity to get to the place where equal access to opportunities exists, as in the case of blind auditions.

For decades, top orchestras auditioned musicians while being able to see them, and they weren't picking women because of the gender biases that exist in our society. Likewise, it has taken over *three decades* for the needle to move only 30%. Why? Because there are other systemic barriers that exist, barriers which cause women to have less *access* to become a top musician in the first place.

If gender bias exists at the top level of the orchestras, it certainly exists every step along the way to get to that level. In high school auditions, acceptance into a performance-based college, opportunity to play for lower-level orchestras, and having the funds to purchase a musical instrument in the first place—the barriers exist every step of the way until that musician can make it to those top positions.

Not all of the steps to musical mastery include equitable rocks like blind auditions. Barriers exist for marginalized groups every step of the way to secure these top orchestra seats, as well as for other jobs, which limit access to equal opportunities.

In life, we cannot always enact a form of a blind audition. We can't just throw a curtain up over all of the systemic issues that exist and say, "Okay, now just work hard." This is the reason a true meritocracy is a lovely concept in theory, but in practice, will not foster equal opportunities for all.

Not yet.

We need the work of equity to dismantle the biases and correct our systems and our processes first so that they truly are working for all. At the same time, we need to also tear down the fence. When that fence is gone, and everyone can see the beauty beyond with equal access to opportunities, only then can we hope to have a meritocracy.

DISPARATE-IMPACT LIABILITY

Now, let's look at a second term that has recently been discussed in the same conversations as meritocracy; and that is "disparate-impact liability."

Disparate-Impact Liability – policies or practices that do not intentionally discriminate, but that have a different (and disadvantageous) impact on one group of employees over another. These groups include gender, race, sexual identity, religion, persons with disabilities, etc.

> At the pure definition of the word, you don't want to disadvantage <u>anyone</u>, ensuring that the processes and practices you have in place are fair, unbiased, and equitable for all.

Some people mistakenly believe that any form of differential treatment violates the Constitution. However, the Civil Rights Act explicitly prohibits disparate treatment, while disparate impact liability is a separate legal doctrine.[23]

Disparate treatment refers to intentional discrimination, where an employer treats individuals differently based on race, gender, or other protected characteristics. This is clearly prohibited under laws like Title VII of the Civil Rights Act of 1964.

Disparate impact, on the other hand, involves seemingly neutral policies that disproportionately affect certain groups, even if there was no intent to discriminate. This concept was recognized by the Supreme Court in Griggs v. Duke Power Co. (1971).[24]

To explain further, I would like to speak to the law.

Title VII of the *Civil Rights Act* says you cannot discriminate based on someone's protected class (their identity).[25] Further, the Equal Employment Opportunity Commission (EEOC) speaks to these protected classes saying, "applicants, employees, and former employees are protected from employment discrimination based on race, color, religion, sex (including pregnancy, sexual orientation, or transgender status), national origin, age (40 or older), disability and genetic information (including family medical history)."[26]

This means that workplaces and educational institutions have processes to safeguard against discrimination taking place for <u>any</u> class—this includes disparate treatment.

As an example, let's take a look at how safeguards born from the work of equity are in place to ensure no disparate treatment or disparate impact is present in hiring, promotion, or layoff processes.

John is a leader in an organization that makes toys for children. The organization has only 500 people and 50% are women and 50% are men. He is going to be expanding his managerial staff, so he needs to hire 10 additional managers. He believes he has the talent to promote from within the organization to fill these roles.

John meets with the recruiting and staffing specialist to fully understand the promotion process before putting it in place. When he gets to the hiring process, he ends up with 30 candidates to interview and they are all males. He didn't mean to do it.

John followed the process that was put in place within his organization. It was unintentional, but because the process yielded all male candidates for the interviews with an organization that is 50% women, somehow the process put women candidates at a disadvantage. This means that there was a problem within the process that needed to be examined.

This is an example of disparate-impact liability.

Now, let's go one step further in this example to understand the term a bit more by describing what would happen next. John reaches out to the Recruiting and Staffing Specialist at his company, and together they analyze their process to see where it failed, and how and where they could do better. What do they do in this situation? The answer might surprise you.

Math.

For both promotion practices and layoff practices, it is typical for Human Resources departments to look at this process and do a statistical analysis—called adverse impact analysis. This ensures the practices are fair and just and are not unintentionally advantageous to any group over another.

Adverse impact analysis is a process that:

- Utilizes metrics to identify discriminatory effects on individuals within protected classes during various human resource processes.
- The analysis provides a statistical review of employment decisions to determine whether discrimination is indicated.
- Furthermore, it focuses on the effect of a policy or process, rather than the intent behind it, comparing selection rates between different groups (e.g., men and women, different racial groups, older and younger workers).

This is sometimes done within organizations when there is a mass layoff. If the report shows statistically that there could be a propensity for any adverse impact on a protected group, then HR teams have to go back in and analyze the decision-making process of that particular action. *Where has it missed the mark? Where is it not equitable for both those in the majority and in the minority?*

We always aim to protect *all* employees, and we have tools and processes (rocks of equity, like the adverse impact analysis) to ensure that equitable practices are in place so that everyone, no matter their race, gender, identity, or religion, is given equal opportunities in the workplace. This is why I believe it is so important that we continue to do whatever we can within the confines of the law to level the playing field—*before* we seek to restore meritocracy. For I, too, would love to see a world in which we give people opportunities based on their merit alone. But there is much more work to be done before we get to that place.

OUR DIFFERENCES MAKE US HUMAN

I believe the equity disconnect—a fundamental misunderstanding of what equity is and what it isn't— identified in Chapter One is becoming more pronounced in today's global society. If "equitable" processes are being equated to promoting women, people of color, LGBTQ+, and other minority groups at the *disadvantage* of white men, the word and the work are not fully understood.

At its core, disparate impact states that we don't want to disadvantage *anyone*. It says that you do the statistical analyses to ensure that the processes and practices you have in place are fair, unbiased, and <u>equitable</u> for *all*—both those in the minority and those in the majority. In other words, equitable processes like the adverse impact analysis give all employees equitable treatment (the rocks—in our rocks and fence analogy) so that everyone can see over the fence.

As we know from Chapter Two, equity is not, in fact, synonymous with preferential treatment but that it can be viewed as such where there is complete denial that the fence (systemic issues and isms—sexism, racism, homophobia, etc.) even exists. This denial (or misunderstanding) is why I believe tensions have risen so high from 2020 forward.

But I do not believe that a meritocracy is the path to move us toward equality of opportunity. Equity is.

Why? Because it is a fact that people are *different*. I wish we lived in a world where this was celebrated instead of scorned. But it is a fact that cannot be changed. So, we must consider our differences (gender, sexual orientation, race, access to education, our class, our zip codes, etc.) when building out new policies and analyzing existing ones. We must continue to ask, *Is this truly for all?* Instead of just telling everyone to "work harder" as meritocracy suggests.

That "work harder" mindset does not bridge the gap, meaning it does not level the playing field. It certainly does not allow us all to see over the fence or have equal opportunities to strive for what we desire most.

People are inherently unique. We come from all walks of life, different cultures, and different circumstances. Our differences are a core part of our humanity. But they are also why we can't make blanket statements and say, "May the best person win".

We do not all start from the same place, with the same resources, or with the same access. The best person, in many cases, is not the one who works the hardest, because when <u>access</u> is limited and implicit biases are present in the decision-making process, who is working the "hardest" doesn't matter.

WE NEED EQUITY *FIRST*

If we do away with the work of equity—work like our statistical analyses to safeguard against disparate impact and ensure workplace practices are indeed equitable— decisions will simply be made on the basis of: *Who does the person doing the hiring <u>believe</u> is the most qualified person?*

That is why equity must come <u>first</u> so we can meet people where they are, and so that everyone can actually have whatever they aspire to have. Put another way, they get the job they want because they work hard for it, and they do not face obstacles or barriers in the process. In order to achieve this "true meritocracy," we have to take out the bias which causes some of these obstacles and barriers within the hiring process.

Let's dive into a practical example of what the work of equity looks like and how it helps us to level the playing field.

These are some specific equitable practices (the work) that have been implemented into the hiring processes in many large corporations and small businesses alike to make the process as unbiased as possible.

1. **Blind Resumes:** Also called resume scrubbing. This is where the recruiter takes off any descriptors that might identify if a candidate is male, female, a

person of color, their age, gender identity, etc. This is so that bias is taken out for the person who is reviewing the resumes and deciding who to bring in for the interview.

This could include descriptors such as being president of a fraternity or sorority, which signifies gender. And be replaced with "president of a Greek organization" so that the gender bias is removed. The valuable experience and unique perspective of the candidate remain the focal point.

2. **Structured Interviewing:** This is where you have set "interview guides" so that each and every candidate that is interviewed is asked the same questions based on this guide. This way, internal biases and systemic biases are removed from the question set.

Having structured interview questions also prevents interviewers from asking questions that could lead to discrimination based on protected characteristics under laws such as the Civil Rights Act, Americans with Disabilities Act (ADA), and Age Discrimination in Employment Act (ADEA).

Some examples of illegal interview questions include:

- **Age**
"How old are you?"

"What year did you graduate from high school?"

- **Marital or Family Status**
"Are you married?"

"Do you have kids or plan to?"
"Who will take care of your children while you're at work?"

- **Nationality or Citizenship**
  "Where were you born?"
  "What is your native language?"
  "Are you a U.S. citizen?"

  (<u>Note</u>: Employers can ask if you are legally authorized to work in the U.S.)

- **Religion**
  "What religion do you practice?"
  "Do you attend church regularly?"
  "Can you work on weekends or religious holidays?"
  (Without a job-related reason.)

- **Disability or Health Status**
  "Do you have any disabilities?"
  "Have you ever been hospitalized?"
  "Do you take any medications?"

  (<u>Note:</u> They can ask if you can perform specific job functions, with or without reasonable accommodation.)

- **Gender Identity or Sexual Orientation**
  "What is your gender?"
  "Are you gay or straight?"

- **Race or Ethnicity**
  "What race are you?"
  "What's your ethnic background?"

- **Financial Status**
  "Do you own your home?"
  "Have you ever declared bankruptcy?"

  (<u>Note</u>: Only relevant in very limited cases, like financial services roles.)

- **Arrest Record**
  "Have you ever been arrested?"

Structured interview guides ensure no illegal questions or biased gender, race, disability, religion, etc. questions are asked from any internal prejudices or even a lack of understanding or education around certain sensitive topics that may be asked out of curiosity or judgment. It ensures equal opportunities to move on to the next step of the hiring process based on a candidate's answers to the interview guide questions alone. This helps us to find the "best candidate for the job" by comparing answers to the same question set.

3. **Panel Interviews:** Instead of interviewing one-on-one, where Interviewer #1 speaks with the candidate, and then they're interviewed by Interviewer #2, and then by Interviewer #3, in panel interviews, all interviewers sit on a panel together.

   This means that they are all interviewing the candidate at the same time, using their interview guide from point #1 above. Panel interviews banish the "he said she said" that can sometimes arise during the interview process, because everyone is hearing the candidate's responses at the same time, asking the same questions, and asking for clarification wherever it is needed. So when the interviewers have their meeting to discuss the candidates, they can talk in a much more constructive and unbiased way because, even if they interpreted the candidate's responses differently, they can talk about it together, and it fosters a more collaborative and unbiased approach.

You can see how these three examples of rocks of equity work toward a level playing field for *all*. It supports both those in the majority and in the minority to receive access to the same opportunities.

- Resumes are read purely from an experience perspective, with biases taken out.
- Questions are not based on an interviewer's internal biases, but are instead from a comprehensive and equitable guide that asks everyone the same questions.
- Interview panels help interviewers and candidates alike to be better supported by our unique and varied perspectives, taking out the bias of one single opinion to foster a more collaborative interview process.

These rocks of equity can help us work towards a meritocracy. But without equity, we cannot hope to move to a place where everyone has equal access to opportunities without barriers or obstacles standing in the way of one or more groups. We cannot remove equity from the conversation and simply cross our fingers and hope that equal opportunities will be had for all. We have to do the work to dismantle our systemic biases, structures, and processes that are not for all, and make them so.

That's why I believe that we need the work of equity now more than ever to help us level the playing field so that we may all have the opportunity to see over the fence, even in a merit-based system.

CHAPTER SIX

IS "FAIR" JUST A PLACE YOU GO TO LOOK AT LIVESTOCK AND EAT FUNNEL CAKE?

FAIRNESS ISN'T ENOUGH <u>ON</u> ITS OWN

We now know why equity is necessary even through the lens of a merit-based system. Now let's talk about the next approach that hasn't worked to bring about true progress—**fairness.**

We touched briefly on fairness in Chapter Three, when we debunked the misunderstanding that fairness is synonymous with equality. Equity and fairness are closely related, yes, but they aren't quite the same. Let us refer back to our definitions from that chapter for a quick refresher.

> **Equality** means that everyone—regardless of age, gender, sexual orientation, or ethnic background—receives <u>the same </u>resources and opportunities.

Equality = treating everyone the same regardless of individual differences or circumstances.

Fairness means doing what's right to ensure everyone has <u>equal access</u>, based on the context of the situation. Access is the key differentiator here. Since we're all starting from different places, access for one person may be different for someone else.

Fairness = giving people what they need to succeed, even if that means treating people differently in order to reach a just outcome.

We then took it a step further to define how equity incorporates fairness.

Equity is defined as being fair and just in the way that people are treated. This treatment, while free from bias or favoritism, tailors support to individual needs so that everyone can have access to the opportunities they need to thrive.

Equity = actions done to tailor support to individual needs, which enables fairness.

Now, let's clarify our definitions even further.

Equity and fairness are closely related, yes, but they aren't quite the same. Fairness is a broader concept—it is the idea that people should be treated justly, without favoritism or bias. But what is "fair" can mean different things to different people. Sometimes it means giving everyone the same thing (equality). Sometimes it means accounting for differences.

Equity, on the other hand, is more specific. It means giving people what they need to succeed, even if that means treating them differently. Equity recognizes that not everyone starts from the same place, and aims to correct these imbalances.

For example: fairness might mean giving everyone the same pair of shoes. While equity means, giving everyone a pair of shoes that actually fit.

Whenever I encounter a misunderstanding that continues to persist, I know it is something that needs to be explored in greater detail. This is the reason I want to dive deeper into fairness in this chapter and draw the connection to how it relates to equity. Let's look at it through the lens of a question I get asked all too often:

"Isn't treating everyone the same <u>fair</u>?"

My short answer? No, it is not. My longer, more detailed answer? Let's explore that now.

As a young girl, my father always used to say, "*Celeste, fair is a place you go to look at pigs,*" as in a county fair, a state fair, or a place you go to judge pigs in show. You'll see what exactly he meant shortly. Put another way, "fair" as in fairness is interpreted differently depending on a person's specific vantage point. Because what one person defines as fair can be entirely different from what another sees as fair in the same situation.

From my father's perspective as a Black man who grew up in early 1900s America and then went on to be the first Black teacher in his school district, and then the first Black principal, his experiences and the things he faced throughout his life had been far from fair. To him, adversity was a common occurrence, so the word "fair" meant nothing to him beyond a literal place of entertainment where you go to see animals put up for show, enjoy carnival games, and gorge yourself with sweet treats.

Likewise, across companies and industries, if I had a dollar for every time I heard—"*But, Celeste, that's not fair*" over my forty years of experience as an HR leader... Well, let's just say I would be a very *very* rich woman. Because fairness?

It's subjective.

In other words, fairness is based on your personal perspective and experiences, and it varies from person to person. To illustrate this, let's say Joe and Mary both apply for the same job. Mary gets the job, and Joe doesn't. Even though it was a fully equitable interview process that incorporated blind resumes, a structured interviewing guide, and panel interviews (like we discussed in the last chapter), Joe doesn't think it's fair that he didn't get the job and Mary did.

Equitable practices like a structured interview process take as much unconscious bias out as possible—such as biases including gender, age, physical appearance, or identity. But you can't fully take out human bias or personal, subjective feelings.

Which means that yes, it is Joe's prerogative to feel that he should have gotten a job he was qualified for—even if he wasn't the most qualified among all the candidates. But it also means that what is and isn't "fair" in this case is Joe's *opinion*. Since the job interview was conducted in an entirely equitable manner, and Mary had a few more qualifications than Joe did (that he wasn't aware of), the concept of fairness is going to differ from person to person here. But that doesn't discount the fact that the panel of interviewers made a decision based on their set guidelines and equitable practices about who would be the best candidate, or that Mary will do a fantastic job in her new position.

We can also see this grey area around fairness play out in our day-to-day life when it comes to sibling dynamics. As a mother, I tried as best I could to have fair and equitable practices with my children. But it could be quite the challenge because, as parents, we're also dealing with society. I have one boy and one girl, and society often says a boy "should be" the one taking out the garbage and the girl "should be" the one washing dishes. Instead, my husband and I chose to have both children learn to do both things, and we would see who was better at which, and who liked which task more. Still, I heard *"But Mom, that's not fair!"* countless times. As children grow and get older, equitable practices are easier to implement, but fairness often remains in the eye of the beholder.

To illustrate this, all of my fellow parents out there will know this scenario well. Or if you're not a parent, but grew up with siblings, I'm sure you faced something similar countless times growing up. I know I did.

You're a parent to Sally (5 years old) and Sam (4 years old). You're in the other room, so you can't see what's going on. Suddenly, you hear screaming from that other room, and you know you have to go break up whatever sibling rivalry scenario is playing itself out. When you ask Sally and Sam what happened, each child has a different opinion. // *He pushed me first, Mom!* // *No, I didn't. Plus, she stole my toy.* // *It's my toy, I had it first!!* //

You ask Sally to give Sam back his toy because that's only fair if he was playing with it, and she, in fact, grabbed it from his hands. Sam is happy to get his toy back, and he feels that your decision is fair. While Sally feels that the toy has been taken away from her, and that you asking her to give the toy back is unfair.

Sound familiar?

This fairness in the eyes of the beholder can play out in countless ways. When you have to divvy up something amongst your children, or you have to send one to school because the other child is sick, but your oldest doesn't understand why she has to go to school when her younger sibling doesn't.

Although the scenarios are endless, as a parent, your task remains the same: treat your children fairly. We have the same intention in the workplace, to treat all of our employees fairly.

However, just because you, as the parent, perceive an outcome of a situation as "fair", definitely doesn't mean both of your children will agree with you. If we take a similar situation and apply it to the workforce with your employees, this same concept holds true as well. But that's only because fairness is subjective to the individual. That is why we have to qualify fairness with equitable practices. So we are giving everyone equal access to opportunities that exist, instead of leaving subjective "fairness" up to the eye of the beholder.

How Classism and Economics Shape Fair

To look at it another way, a world of true fairness would be like the 100-meter race, where everyone starts at the starting line, is positioned at the ready on their starting blocks, and is wearing their new set of running shoes (called "spikes" for track Mom's like me). The official says, *"On your marks, set!"* then fires the starting pistol and the race begins. How well you do in life in this scenario is simply based on how fast you run and how quickly you get to that finish line. We all start at the same starting line and end at the same finish. However well you place in the race is based solely on how hard you worked (meritocracy), and the outcome is fair to all.

Now think of it this way. In our current reality, a handful of people get to start at the starting line. A few more are set 10 meters back, others start from 20 meters back, and a few of the runners don't even have running spikes. Our circumstances and differences *matter* because they determine our starting line and who has, or doesn't have, that new pair of spikes to support them as they run throughout the race that is life. Equity asks that we recognize these differences and then provide support to ensure everyone can reach the finish line fairly.

To reflect further on our different starting points, let's look at an example of how classism and economics shape opportunity and fairness in our current world. You'll have heard the common phrase—*they were born with a silver spoon in their mouth.* Meaning that person was born into a wealthy family with the advantages that come with having a privileged upbringing. The phrase is thrown about often, but what are the actual real-world implications of being born with or without that silver spoon?

For one, neighborhoods matter. In conventionally higher-income neighborhoods such as the Upper East Side in Manhattan, access to opportunities often starts before one is even born. Getting your child into a premier preschool is seen as the impetus (a necessity) for your child to have access to the best private primary school and high school education. Waitlists are long, and preschool fees approach $40,000 per year, with parents often fighting to get their child on the waitlist before they are even born. Only if the child continues on this track from "cradle to Columbia" can the parents rest easy that their child will have the education and qualifications necessary to secure their spot at an Ivy League university, which will then lead to their choice of top jobs upon graduation.[27]

On the other hand, children born into lower-income zip codes face systematic disadvantages from the start. They face underfunded schools, fewer resources, overworked teachers, meager access to programs like the arts and other extracurricular activities, and limited access to assistance for students with disabilities and special education needs. Data from the Child Poverty Action Group says that "children from lower-income households [are] less likely to achieve than their more affluent peers. This results in unequal life chances and futures, with children growing up in poverty earning less as adults."[28]

The disparities between education in lower-income neighborhoods versus higher-income neighborhoods can, and do, impact short and long-term student outcomes. When teachers face class sizes upwards of thirty students, they simply cannot dedicate the same personalized time and attention to each student. Many schools don't have enough textbooks for each student to learn, or lack textbooks with updated content because they do not have the funding to access the most up-to-date print. Likewise, students from lower-income areas often have limited, or no, access to computers and technology to learn in the modern age. The discrepancy in resources between underfunded schools versus well-funded institutions is vast, and our children, and their education, are greatly impacted by it. Impact doesn't end in elementary school, high school, or university, but has long-term repercussions that influence job opportunities and earning potential in the future.

As you can see, our starting line is often determined before we are even born, and we do not all begin from the same place or circumstances. This "starting line" has lasting effects throughout our lives with systemic, financial, and educational barriers holding back bright minds from all walks of life.

Life is not fair. And while we can commit ourselves to doing the work to provide fair and just opportunities for all, that work is not simply sitting back and hoping for fairness—it is doing the work of *equity*. It is enacting the policies and practices to help our marginalized groups and individuals move from their starting blocks set 10 or 20 meters behind the starting line up to more equal footing with their more advantaged peers, so that opportunities to thrive are available for all.

In schools in lower-income neighborhoods, this work of equity could look like:

Providing free meals at school. Hungry children are not only unable to concentrate on their studies, but can also face health effects such as malnourishment. Providing free school meals is a rock of equity to remove a basic but critical barrier to focus, behavior, and academic performance. Every child deserves nourishment and education, regardless of their background or circumstances.

Support with school costs. Find ways to provide lower-income families access to additional school costs like pens, pencils, laptops, uniforms, and more. This ensures that all students can participate fully and confidently in school activities, reducing feelings of exclusion or shame due to appearance or affordability. It also reduces financial strain on parents and eases the emotional and logistical load on teachers who often must step in to support students lacking the necessary supplies to learn.

Education should not be conditional on wealth or circumstances, and it is the work of equity that is needed to work towards fairness.

FAIR AND EQUITABLE PRACTICES

Both our workplace example with Joe and Mary and those

infamous sibling dynamics illustrate why fairness language alone is insufficient, both examples reinforce why the word equity must remain central in our conversations and practices.

Fairness is subjective. Equity is the work in action.

In Human Resources, many people will use *Fair and Equitable Processes* as a single term to incorporate the work of equity (the processes and policies) with the sentiment of fairness (tailoring support to individual needs). I am okay with this, so long as the actual word "equity" remains in the conversation. Why? Because equity strives to be fair and just in the way that people are treated, yes. But it then takes the concept of fairness a step further to remove bias and favoritism and ensure equal access to opportunities.

Put another way, equity is the checks and balances, the actual processes and practices (such as the structured interview process we outlined in Chapter Five) that move us towards lasting, equitable progress.

For that reason, let us now adjust our definition of equity from Chapter Three to include the term *fair and equitable,* so that we may highlight its relationship to equity as a whole.

> **Equity** is defined as being fair and just in the way that people are treated. This treatment, while free from bias or favoritism, tailors support to individual needs so that everyone can have access to the opportunities they need to thrive.

> **Fair and Equitable** = *providing resources to enable everyone to have access to opportunities, whatever those opportunities may be (access to jobs, food, homes, etc.)*

Moreover, it is fair and equitable practices that provide equal access by tailoring support to individual needs. From this, you can see that without equity as part of the fairness language, systemic barriers continue, and outcomes and opportunities remain unequal. Because when everyone is treated "the same," without consideration of where they started from and the daily barriers they face, we cannot hope to have true fairness.

CHAPTER SEVEN

THE DEI CONTINUUM—WHY DO WE NEED DIVERSITY, EQUITY, AND INCLUSION?

BRINGING INCLUSION INTO THE DIVERSITY CONVERSATION

I now want to briefly bring diversity and inclusion of Diversity, Equity, and Inclusion (DEI) to the forefront of our equity conversation. For a more detailed discussion on both diversity and inclusion, I encourage you to pick up my first book. But for the context of our discussion here, we are using the terms in the following context.

Diversity is differences in people, both those you can see and those you can't see.

Inclusion is actively creating spaces where all can participate.

There are three steps here to understand the importance of Diversity, Equity, and Inclusion as a whole:

1. Because people are different, you need **equity** (or equitable practices) to meet people where they are and leverage the inherent diversity of our world.
2. **Diversity** leveraged in an optimal manner helps us come together to reach a collective purpose.
3. A culture of **inclusion** is then needed to facilitate an organization's collective purpose, where everyone is able to contribute toward that purpose.

This is why all three components of DEI—diversity, equity, and inclusion—are incredibly important in bringing about progress within our society. That includes our workplaces, educational institutions, nonprofits, public sectors, and all teams within them.

In any workplace, success is about being able to perform as a team and perform well towards the mission of the company, it's not only about diversity. You can have a work team that is diverse in how they think, in their perspectives, in different backgrounds, cultures, and experiences—and still fall short.

Simply having a diverse team is not enough. You must *leverage* those differences to achieve the desired outcome. By this I mean, putting your team's valuable and varied experiences, beliefs, values, ideas, and perspectives towards a common and collective goal—that's where inclusion and diversity come into play within the work of equity.

Think of leveraging the diversity of your team like

making a stew. You have all the ingredients to make a delicious stew—the beef, carrots, celery, broth, and spices. And ultimately, you want it to taste good. But without bringing all of these ingredients together and then leveraging them (by simmering them at the exact right temperature, for the exact right amount of time), you will not have a stew.

You must cultivate your team in the same way. Just as you add all of the varied ingredients into the stew, everyone on your team needs to be able to add their individual and unique value to contribute to the team's overall success.

Taking it a step further, you won't have inclusion by treating everyone the same. For example, Aaron, who is a single parent of a special needs child has to leave work every day at a certain time to be with his child. But once he gets home and settles his child in, he can work from his home office to complete any assignments. As a leader, you are meeting Aaron where he is, not treating him the same as everyone else, but by allowing him to manage his time appropriately *while* still contributing to the team.

Similarly, you do not have a delicious stew by adding the same amount of each ingredient to the pot. There is a recipe for success. Because my needs are different from my colleagues' needs and vice versa, we can't be treated the exact same way and expect to produce our most innovative thinking and work. For this reason, leaders need to be able to meet each member of their team where they are so that everyone has a chance to contribute their full voice to the conversation, like we saw in our example with Aaron. I will clarify in more detail what this looks like in the next section.

As a leader, it's asking: *Okay, our equitable practices (like the structured interview process or blind auditions, both outlined in Chapter Five) have successfully helped us to build a diverse team. Now, how do we take those differences and leverage them for the collective purpose?*

YOUR COMPANY AND YOUR CUSTOMERS

When the D (diversity) and the E (equity) are in place, the next step is I (inclusion). It is asking leadership questions like these and then actively creating an environment that capitalizes on all the varied knowledge you have on your team.

It's important to understand that "knowledge" can take many forms. It might come from formal education, personal experiences, cultural background, or expertise in different fields. Each person gains knowledge in unique ways, shaped by where they learned, how they learned, and the perspectives they bring from their learning.

For example: If one person on your team has experience in sales, another in marketing, and a third in market research, you want to be able to include all of their varying perspectives and expertise to work towards your desired outcome. In addition, bringing diverse cultural experiences to the table is an invaluable asset to any team.

Why? No matter what your company does, most likely your customers come from a wide range of backgrounds. When your internal teams are just as diverse, they bring different cultural perspectives that help your company better understand and connect with your customers and their experiences.

An example of this sentiment that I love is an urban myth often used in Human Resources to explain the importance of building diverse teams. It's a story I heard over thirty years ago when I first started working in HR, and is one I want to tell you.

Back in the 1960s, the Chevrolet *Nova* car was released. A brand new, compact car was hitting sales floors worldwide. When the Chevy marketing team was deciding on the perfect name that would convey the essence of the car, sell well to their customers, and exemplify strong branding, they landed on the name... *Nova*. When the car was officially released, customers loved it. But for some reason, the car wasn't selling well with their Latino and Spanish-speaking customers. The team could not figure out why.

Turns out, in Spanish, *Nova* or "no va" quite literally means "doesn't go." Who wants to buy a new car that tells you right in the name that it doesn't go anywhere? Nobody. Can you imagine the leader of that marketing team getting the sales report back and the company's CEO asking, *What happened? Did you not have someone who knows how to speak Spanish on your team?* Then, having to answer "No." I can only imagine what that conversation was like between those two leaders.

Without a diverse team that leverages everyone's unique skills and insight (like someone who speaks the primary language of a large portion of your customer base), it is easy to make an uninformed decision on something as simple as what to call your product. Your team should reflect the real-world demographics and population of your customers. Not just the majority, but all of them. There is immense value in diverse teams that reflect the world we live in—not only to the bottom line of our companies, but also to the innovative work of the individual teams themselves.

THE STRENGTH OF DIVERSE TEAMS

A common leadership myth I see, and perhaps an objection you may even have as you're reading this, is that diverse teams underperform. When, in fact, diverse teams go through a natural adjustment phase—like any other team—a phase that is necessary to get to peak performance.

In his *Forming, Storming, Norming, and Performing* model, psychologist Bruce Tuckman posits that to enhance team effectiveness there are four stages:[29]

- Forming – where the team is first brought together, roles are defined, and everyone meets.
- Storming – where conflicts naturally arise as everyone's strengths are determined and team members push boundaries.
- Norming – this is the stage where differences begin to be seen as a benefit and collaboration increases.

Performing – when a team has reached peak performance and is outputting valuable results.

For any team, conflicts arise and then are resolved, in order to make space for true collaboration to grow. Diverse teams go through this same adjustment period, so that they can perform and operate at their highest efficiency. But with strong leadership, diverse teams actually <u>outperform</u> in the long run because their varied perspectives and skills have been leveraged to benefit the team's output. I believe it is the leader's job to foster and leverage inclusion to get diverse teams to that stage of peak performance. And not blame diversity for the natural adjustment period required of any newly formed team. Let's dive into a few examples that support this point.

Companies that are committed to Diversity, Equity, and Inclusion regularly outperform companies that do not have DEI policies and procedures in place. Diversity has been linked with more significant revenue growth and more satisfied employees. A study from McKinsey & Company, *Diversity Matters Even More* looked at 1,265 companies, 23 countries, and six global regions and found that diversity on executive teams *increased* the likelihood of financial outperformance by 25% on gender diverse teams and 36% on teams with diverse ethnic representation. While teams that were not as diverse were significantly less likely to financially outperform (decreasing a company's profitability).[30]

Likewise, a study from Boston Consulting Group of 1,700 companies across eight countries found that diverse teams had 19% higher *innovation revenue*, or revenue from products launched within the past three years.[31]

An article from Forbes in 2017, highlighted a study using the Cloverpop decision-making database found that diverse teams saw an increase in decision-making accuracy. Teams that were diverse in age, gender, and geography made better business decisions at all levels 87% of the time.[32] Teams that followed an inclusive process made decisions two times faster, and with half the number of meetings.

When people come to me and say that diverse teams don't perform well, I challenge them with: *Is that the team's fault or the leader's fault?* And I will do the same here today. The best outcome from a diverse team is going to come when you leverage inclusion. When the team leader creates a space where everyone can participate using their unique skills, gleaned from diverse backgrounds and perspectives, performance goes up.

That is why the work of equity is so important within the context of Diversity, Equity, and Inclusion. We can't reach our full potential as organizations unless we do the work to create equity. Without it, companies miss out on the talents of people who haven't had the same opportunities as others—especially those whose life experiences have made it harder to access a seat at the table. To truly succeed, we need to level the playing field so that everyone has a chance to contribute their valuable perspectives.

Put more simply, to harness a diverse team's potential in order to drive home whatever outcome you are looking to achieve, you must have inclusion. If any one person on the team feels left out, then you are not benefiting from their enriched experience, understanding, and voice.

THE JOURNEY OF DIVERSITY, EQUITY, AND INCLUSION

I believe that equity is the key to fostering fairness and justice, so that we can make sure that everyone has what they need to succeed, in our workplaces and beyond.

When we look at it from the standpoint of the Diversity, Equity, and Inclusion continuum we discussed at the beginning of this chapter, we can see how equity helps us achieve inclusion and fairness in diverse workplaces. As a reminder,

1. People have differences; that's diversity. Those differences are based on their culture, experiences in life, and where they were born.
2. On the other side, there is inclusion. Inclusion helps teams work better together to come up with fresh ideas and to stay more engaged because everyone feels valued. An inclusive environment attracts great people, who will in turn make smarter decisions and build a positive reputation.
3. When people are surrounded by a culture of inclusion, they can be more innovative, more creative, increase their output, and get better outcomes (as we saw in the statistics on diverse teams above).

But achieving this is easier said than done, and it is quite the journey from our differences as a starting point, to a culture of inclusion. To close the gap, we have to perform acts of equity by setting up practices and processes to tailor to individual needs in a way that is free from bias and favoritism. While performing acts of equity (the rocks), you must also continue to do the ongoing work of breaking down the systemic barriers (the fence). We have to do this work to get to inclusion—and to the innovation and success that inclusion in the workplace can produce.

Part of that work is understanding the differences in people, meeting them where they currently are at point A and asking: *What do you need to get to point Z? What are the obstacles currently standing in your way of successfully getting there?*

The answer is unique to each individual. The answer is based upon where they are and where they've come from through their life experience. But we'll never be able to get them to point Z (where the fence is torn down and everyone can see the beauty beyond) if we refuse to understand those differences, refuse to see the obstacles that stand in the way, and ignore the necessary work to remove the barriers ("isms": sexism, homophobia, racism) that prevent everyone from having equal access to opportunities.

We see the varied answers to what exactly people need everywhere. An example is inequities that exist within our health care systems. The COVID-19 Pandemic shined a light on these inequities when we saw firsthand that not everyone had equal access to healthcare. Take something as simple as when the COVID vaccine was finally made available in the United States. The vaccine had the *potential* to be accessible to all (regardless of socioeconomic status), but was it?

The National Library of Medicine conducted a study on the COVID vaccine distribution and found that "across the

US 16.3% of adults and 37.9% of adults aged 65 and older were vaccinated in lower [socioeconomic status] counties, while 20.5% of all adults and 48.16% of adults aged 65 and older were vaccinated in higher [socioeconomic status] counties. Inequalities emerged after forty-one days when less than 2% of Americans were vaccinated."[33] This means that social inequalities (like access to health insurance and nearby local pharmacies) reflected an "inequitable distribution" of vaccine delivery and that the imbalance could be seen after less than 2% of the total population was vaccinated.

Just like health equity, the COVID-19 Pandemic also shined a light on inequities in education. When students were moved to online classes and learning at home, it quickly became apparent that not everyone had access to the tools required to learn outside of a classroom setting. I'll never forget seeing pictures of young students with their moms and dads sitting on the sidewalk outside of a Starbucks or another neighborhood store that had free Wi-Fi on their parents' phones, attempting to complete their schoolwork because they didn't have internet access or laptops at home.

The inequities that we saw during the Pandemic, based on someone's social and economic condition, were emotionally paralyzing and disheartening. But my biggest takeaway from that time was the number of people who said, *"I just didn't know."* It is so easy to remain in our own little worlds, our own comfortable social bubbles, and not realize that there is a whole other reality just beyond our doorsteps—where real people don't have access to simple things like Wi-Fi, laptops, and the healthcare that we take for granted.

I am not sharing this to place any blame, but to remind us of a time when the fences and barriers that hold others back were more clearly seen. I want to encourage us not to forget those times. Although the headlines are different now and the emphasis on inequities in our systems aren't as visible, they still remain.

It is only when we strip away the veil of misunderstanding from our eyes and educate ourselves around the work that needs to be done (just as you are doing by reading this book) that we can hope to get to that culture of inclusion. A culture that ultimately allows everybody to experience the positive outcomes that we want, both in business and education, and in our societies as a whole.

It is my hope that Parts I and II of this book have given you the tools of education to help you move forward— whether at work or in your personal life—with a much better understanding of what equity is, its importance, and why we need it now more than ever.

Now that your foundational knowledge around equity is set, let us move on to Part III, where we'll explore equity in action and to see firsthand how it provides advantages for us all.

PART III

CHAPTER EIGHT

EQUITY IN ACTION | EDUCATION AND HEALTHCARE

B efore I jump into equity in action for education and healthcare, I want to first explain how I've structured the next three chapters. We've spoken at length within the pages of this book about what equity really is and what it isn't. Now, in Part III, we are shifting our focus to the *benefits* of equity. I want to reframe equity once and for all, not as a dirty word but as a practical concept. When we get it right, <u>everyone</u> wins.

Because when we get it right, societies as a whole benefit. For example, equity-forward societies are more stable and prosperous, and innovation thrives in diverse, equitable environments. Another of equity's benefits is that it provides not only opportunities to uplift marginalized groups (opportunities which we'll explore below), it also creates a more fulfilling and inclusive environment for everyone. Equity expands opportunities *without* diminishing resources for others.

In the next three chapters, we're going to look closely at how everyone wins when we get equity right, by highlighting real-world examples of how societies and communities <u>benefit</u>. I'll also share stories of how equity has impacted me personally.

In each chapter, I will provide an example of equity in action from countries around the world to illustrate the potential for its impact. When we see firsthand the strong progress that has already been made towards implementing equitable practices in areas like education, healthcare, economic opportunity, and social inclusion, we can better understand equity in action.

In the next three chapters, we will dive deeper into equity's role in providing:

1. **Advantages for marginalized groups**, which include: access to opportunities, improved quality of life, empowerment and dignity, and the reduction of discrimination.

2. **Advantages for those in the majority**, which include: enhanced social stability, increased innovation and creativity, economic growth, fairer workplaces and communities, and broadened understanding and empathy.

3. **Shared advantages for both groups** (both those in the minority and those in the majority), which include: stronger communities, better decision-making, healthier societies, and moral and ethical progress.

Let's explore these advantages now beginning with education and healthcare systems.

MY PERSONAL ROCK OF EQUITY

As I mentioned in Chapter Six, my father was the first Black teacher in western Pennsylvania, and the school where he taught was about 50% Black or persons of color and 50% white and Italian—the most diverse school in our small Pennsylvania steel mill town. When he became Assistant Principal, he saw firsthand how hard it was to get the same resources for his school that were readily available at the nearby school where I attended. This was a majority white school that my parents chose very specifically because of the opportunities that it would afford me. I champion my mother and father for understanding firsthand the differences that equitable education opportunities afford children, and then advocating for access for me.

In the public school system, you would think that every school gets allocated the same resources. When, in fact, each state in the U.S. has its own formula for how it distributes funds throughout its school districts. In some more rural areas, all tax dollars go into one pool and are distributed equally, yes. But in most states, public schools receive funding that is paid for through property taxes. So schools in wealthy neighborhoods typically have more funding and resources available because of higher taxes, while lower-income neighborhood schools, where fewer tax resources are present, often receive less.

As a young girl, my school district had very different resources and opportunities available for students than my father's school. From a very young age, I noticed how hard my father needed to advocate for his school to get various items —school programs, textbooks, and learning supplies—that were freely given at the school I attended.

One example readily comes to mind. In elementary school, I had a lisp, a speech impediment, where I had difficulty pronouncing words that started with the "TH" sound as in three, the, and therefore. My father knew that the school I attended had a program available where, two or three days a week, I could walk down from the elementary school over to the high school and work one-on-one with a speech and language therapist for an hour. His school, however, did not have speech classes available for students with speech impediments similar to mine.

I was able to take advantage of school programs like this one for two reasons. First, my school had the resources that made opportunities like correcting a speech impediment possible. Second, my father and mother educated themselves on how the system worked, and made sure they knew what programs were available, and where, and they advocated for me to participate in them.

That speech program was an incredible rock of equity for me. Having a speech impediment can follow you throughout your life, including how you're perceived in the workforce. It can influence job opportunities and more. Because I was given the speech therapy that I uniquely needed at a young age, I was able to begin middle school on an equal playing field with all of my peers, instead of being held back by my lisp. Years later, when I graduated from undergraduate university, I went on to be a reporter, then a high-level executive, and now I speak on stages around the world. This is a career trajectory that would not have been possible without the confidence to speak freely and fully. It's a quality I now hold dear, because I know this life path was made possible by a simple rock of equity within the education system—speech therapy.

Let's broaden the scope to look at how equitable policy changes have been implemented in education and healthcare systems around the world to further outline the benefits of equity in action.

REAL RESULTS FROM AROUND THE WORLD: FINLAND

Equitable practices within school systems have an incredible impact on the lives of our children. Just as I examined my rock of equity in speech therapy, let's look at how equity in education has been implemented in Finland.

Equal Access to Education: Finland's focus on leveling the playing field for all within education gives us a strong real-world example of equity in action. The entire country has enacted policies engineered to tear down the systemic barrier of limited access to education based on financial means.

What They Do Well: Finland's education system is consistently ranked among the best and is world-renowned for equity in action. All students have access to high-quality education <u>regardless</u> of socioeconomic background.

Key Equitable Initiatives In Place: [34]

- **Universal free education.** In Finland, education is publicly funded across <u>all</u> levels. There are no tuition fees for basic or higher education, meaning that there is no financial barrier to accessing education, no matter the socioeconomic status of your family or the zip code you live in.

- **Meals, transportation, and tuition** are provided to all students for free, ensuring that every student has access to get to and from school each day. And no student's learning or focus is impacted by an empty stomach, with daily meals provided for all.
- **Minimal performance testing.** They have done away with most standardized tests and focus instead on well-being and holistic development of every student. Instead, they focus on personalized learning, with small class sizes that allow for individualized attention and differentiated instruction so that each student's unique needs, interests, and strengths are met and then individually evaluated.
- **Equal Access to Qualified Teachers.** All teachers are required to hold a master's degree, and are given flexibility in their curriculum to tailor their teaching methods to suit individual student needs.

The Benefits in Action: With these policies in place, Finnish students—regardless of their socioeconomic status—consistently excel in assessments such as the *Programme for International Student Assessment*, which looks at how education systems prepare students for success. Students report lower stress and greater satisfaction throughout their school years, and when they enter the professional world, they are equipped with the critical thinking and problem-solving skills to thrive in the workforce.

Now let's look at Canada and the equity achieved in its healthcare system.

REAL RESULTS FROM AROUND THE WORLD: CANADA

Just like in education, equity in healthcare contributes to a more thriving society. When everyone has access to not only life-saving medical care but also consistent access to healthcare throughout their lives, there are fewer systemic health issues among disenfranchised groups, and the society as a whole can function better when its people are healthy.

Multicultural Inclusion and Healthcare: Canada offers a publicly funded, universal healthcare system with programs designed for marginalized groups.

What They Do Well: Canada emphasizes multiculturalism and provides universal healthcare to all residents.

Key Equitable Initiatives in Place:

- **Public healthcare is accessible regardless of income.** All residents, regardless of socioeconomic status, have access to the public healthcare system. Whether or not they have healthcare is not dictated by their job or socioeconomic status. *Everyone* has access to the medical care they need.
- **Jordan's Principle.** In 2016, it was determined that Canada's approach to health services for First Na-

tions (Indigenous peoples in Canada who are neither Inuit nor Métis) children was discriminatory; so they leaned into creating equity by establishing Jordan's Principle, to ensure that First Nations children have "substantively equal access to government services, taking into account their distinct circumstances, experiences, and needs."[35] In other words, First Nations children can access public services without delay or denial due to jurisdictional disputes. This policy in no way took away from the majority, because public healthcare is still available for all, it just removed the barriers that this one particular group once faced and opened up access for all.

- **Culturally Competent Care:** Canada prioritizes investments in training and services to make healthcare more inclusive of racial, cultural, and linguistic diversity, including recognition of unique experiences, preferences, religious beliefs, and cultural values. This involves increasing diversity among healthcare providers, training to develop a culturally competent healthcare system, and improving access to personalized care.[36]

The Benefits in Action: Between 2016 and 2025, Canada approved over 8.9 million products, services, and support for First Nations children, including speech therapy, educational support, medical equipment, and mental health services. Likewise, the Canadian Virtual Hospice program, *Living My Culture Program* gives patients peace of mind and comfort during end-of-life care by taking into account a patient's specific cultural traditions and values.[37] This means that their unique needs, based upon such traditions, are honored within the healthcare system, and taken into account in how they're cared for.

WHEN EQUITY IS DONE RIGHT IN EDUCATION AND HEALTHCARE

We've seen the benefits of equity in action from our real-world examples from Finland and Canada. In this section, let's take a look at further benefits, or advantages, beyond these two countries. Throughout the next three chapters, we'll use this section—*When Equity Is Done Right*—to discuss the universal advantages of equity for those in the minority (marginalized groups), those in the majority, and those in both groups (both those in the majority and those in the minority). These advantages can be applied globally, so I invite you to read this section with your own home country, or where you live currently, in mind.

In this chapter specifically, we'll place our focus on the advantages for all through the lens of education and healthcare in order to expand on our discussion above on a more global scale.

Shared Advantages for Those in Both Groups | Healthier Societies

Reduced inequities lead to improved public health, benefiting everyone regardless of background. We can see this through examples like Canada's Jordan's Principle, which recognized the unique needs of First Nations children. This understanding of needs led to a change in policy and procedure. This policy did not take away from the majority, but instead, allowed everyone to benefit wholly from the public healthcare system. Jordan's Principle continues to promote greater health in the entire country because the varied communities that exist within it are seen, understood, and cared for.

Likewise, Finland's education system fosters educated adults who enter the workplace with critical thinking and problem-solving skills that help them to better contribute to the workforce, which has positive effects on society as a whole —both in the happiness of its citizens and in the functioning of its economy. Let's take a deeper look at how those in the minority and those in the majority are positively impacted when equity is done right.

Advantages for Marginalized Groups | Improved Quality of Life + Empowerment and Dignity

Looking at the countries and their policies we've discussed, you can see that by addressing disparities in healthcare, education, and social services, overall well-being is improved, and economic mobility (the ability to improve economic status) increases. When no one person or group is barred from receiving medical care or education, everyone can be a healthy member of society and contribute their unique skills and perspectives as such. We can see how equity in action from Canada and Finland improves the lives of marginalized groups by giving them equal access to the education and healthcare they uniquely need to improve the quality of their lives.

Likewise, equity fosters a sense of belonging, empowerment, and dignity, helping individuals reach their full potential. An example where this doesn't happen, is when teachers treat boys and girl students differently. This is often not intentional but comes from societal biases around gender. For example, praising girls for physical appearance and encouraging "feminine" subjects such as art, instead of championing the content and quality of their work. While boys are more likely to be encouraged to take courses in science and mathematics, typically perceived as more "masculine" subjects.

In every country, including the United States, schools and teachers have the power to be agents of change, empowering students to show up as their full selves by creating gender-inclusive classroom cultures, reflect on gender biases, and "learn to treat students in ways that are consistent with students' identities, as the non-profit organization *ASCD* (Association for Supervision and Curriculum Development) recommends.[38]

Likewise, in the workplace, I've seen firsthand how people were more empowered to speak up when they had opportunities to do so in a way that took into account their personal comfort level. For example, by tailoring support to individual needs when we were working virtually during the COVID-19 Pandemic, people could share their thoughts and engage with the team via video or chat function.

When we called on certain people firsthand, they may not have been comfortable speaking their minds. But when we invited those same people to openly speak via the chat feature, many more employees were empowered to share their opinions. Because of this, they contributed their unique perspectives to the team in a way that we would have missed out on had we not given people multiple ways to speak up.

Advantages for Those in the Majority | Broader Understanding and Empathy

Interactions with people from diverse backgrounds foster cultural awareness, understanding, and empathy. Cultural awareness is the ability to not only recognize and understand the differences and similarities among cultures, but also to appreciate those differences and the unique perspectives and experiences we all hold. This increases empathy because, through understanding of others, we can connect with and celebrate our cultural differences instead of fearing them.

Those in the majority win when people of every group are understood and feel included, because this allows everyone to contribute their complete selves to the benefit of all. You'll remember we saw an example of this in Chapter Seven when we outlined how diverse teams actually outperform non-diverse teams in the long run since valuable and varied perspectives lead to greater output.

Now, let's take a look at how we all win when equity is done right within community initiatives that benefit economic mobility.

CHAPTER NINE

EQUITY IN ACTION | COMMUNITY INITIATIVES AND ECONOMIC MOBILITY

When I was in my 20s, I worked for General Foods in the HR Department. I was transferred and moved every year and a half—still working for the same company but at a different location. This particular time, I was transferred from New Jersey to Jacksonville, Florida. I felt incredibly lucky because the relocation organization within our company moved me; they took care of everything.

They even set up appointments with a realtor for me over the phone prior to moving, where they told me about all the different parts of the new city I'd be living in, neighborhoods I might enjoy, the pros and cons of each.

It sounded like I had some exciting options of neighborhoods to live in, and I was looking forward to trading the frigid temperatures of New Jersey for a Florida beachside lifestyle.

But because these appointments had all taken place over the phone, the realtor's office made these recommendations to me before ever seeing me in person. When it was time for me to tour these neighborhoods, I made the trip down to Jacksonville to meet with the real estate office. As soon as we were meeting in person, face-to-face, suddenly many of the neighborhoods they'd previously recommended to me were no longer options.

At least, not for me.

Somehow, the wealthier zip codes that I'd just "absolutely love" were no longer "an area of Jacksonville I'd be interested in." Even today, I can still feel the judgment and the barriers that were thrown up around where I could live, simply because of the color of my skin.

From that moment forward, the real estate agency became extremely cagey about what parts of the city they were willing to show me. I was forceful, insisting that I wanted to live on the beach and ended up moving into an apartment in Jacksonville Beach. Living there was fine enough, but after about a year, I knew it wasn't for me, and I rented a house inland in Jacksonville proper for the next year on my own. It didn't take me long before I knew I wanted to move back to the beach, but this time, I was going to do things differently with the realty office. I was going to give myself my own rock of equity because I refused to be limited to certain areas for no reason other than the color of my skin—and the prejudices that certain people held surrounding it.

Since I now knew the area, I knew where I wanted to go—Ponte Vedra Beach. For context, Ponte Vedra is a wealthy suburb of Jacksonville, a much more affluent area than Jacksonville Beach. It's where the headquarters of the

PGA tour was located and was known for being the place where wealthy people came to golf.

And it is absolutely beautiful.

This time, I was committed to level the playing field for myself, and to do that, I knew not to go into the real estate office in person. Instead, I called the office and did everything over the phone. They asked me just a few simple questions before the doors opened wide for me:

> *Who do you work for?* General Foods, one of the largest employers in the city.

> *What's your salary?* They were happy with my answer.

> *What's your current zip code?* Where I was renting in Jacksonville proper was a very nice neighborhood, so they were quite satisfied with that answer as well.

The only question left—*In what area do you want to live?* Ponte Vedra Beach.

About a week later, the realtor's office called me up. A wonderful townhouse was ready for me to move into, everything was set to go. All I needed to do was come in and sign the lease. By this point, all the paperwork had been drawn up, and it was too late for the apartment complex to backtrack. The townhouse was mine to rent.

I remember being on that phone call and thinking to myself, *Wow, this must be what it feels like to be a privileged part of the majority.* Because, yes, even though a privileged person would be asked these same questions when applying for a home, what is different is that as a woman of color, the barrier to entry (the type of questions I get asked to qualify myself to be included in more affluent areas) is much higher, simply because of the color of my skin. I needed to put my own rock of equity in place, similar to the blind orchestra auditions we discussed in Chapter Five, so that what I looked like was not a contributing factor towards my application to live there.

I remember this thought, *this must be what it feels like to be privileged,* with crystal clear clarity even today because everything about the process was so easy once I told them my zip code. They didn't ask any of the questions that I'd gotten my whole life—questions that asked me to prove my worth in spaces where people didn't think I belonged as a Black woman. They didn't even ask for my credit score.

I walked into the real estate office, head held high, signed my paperwork, and the next thing I knew, I was living in a beautiful beachfront townhouse. My two experiences with the moving process in the very same city were entirely different. And I witnessed firsthand just how much zip codes matter and the barriers that come from where you were born or where you currently live. And how much those barriers hinder where you want to go.

Sometimes a rock of equity can be as simple as educating yourself about the barriers that exist, and then advocating for yourself to break through them, as I did in Jacksonville. And although we absolutely can, and should, give ourselves (and others) opportunities to level the playing field where we can, on a personal level, we all benefit far more (and far faster) when broader equitable policies exist to support us.

Let's take a look at a few of these types of broader

equitable initiatives now. Similarly to the last chapter, we will use real results of equity done right from around the world—this time from the United States and Finland.

REAL RESULTS FROM AROUND THE WORLD: UNITED STATES

Imagine not being able to have access to certain neighborhoods simply because of what you look like, or because economic mobility feels impossible when education, job title, and salary all play a role in how freely you can access opportunities beyond your current circumstances.

> **Economic Mobility** refers to the ability of a group, family, or individual to improve their economic status. Economic mobility is often measured by income increases.

Economic mobility is a barrier to equal access that stands strong behind the scenes. It is an economic system that makes it difficult to grow beyond your current circumstances, making improvement of your economic status harder. It leaves groups out, those identified by certain zip codes generation after generation. This is why economic mobility is so important, and why community initiatives (acts of equity) have been adopted around the world to help combat this barrier.

Now, let's take a look at equitable initiatives that boost economic mobility by helping disenfranchised groups improve their economic status. Several American cities have implemented equity-focused strategies that led to notable social and economic advancements for residents. Detroit, Michigan, stands as a great example of a city whose leaders have championed inclusive growth (growth that makes economic mobility available to all) and whose residents have benefited as a result.

Detroit, Michigan

What they do well: Mayor Mike Duggan has prioritized racial equity and inclusive economic development in the city. As a result, Detroit has seen significant improvements in housing equity and economic revitalization— improving the economic health of the city and increasing opportunities for economic mobility of residents.

Key Equitable Initiatives and Benefits in Action:[39]

- **Affordable Housing Development.** The city has created over 4,600 affordable units over the course of five years, through over $1 billion in public and private investments. This enhances housing accessibility for residents who would not have the financial means to house themselves in the city otherwise.
- **Tax Foreclosure Reduction.** A city-wide property tax assistance program helped the city see a 95% decrease in tax foreclosures since 2016. It stabilized neighborhoods, increased property values, and kept people in their homes.
- **Home Value Increases.** Thanks to the tax foreclosure reduction initiative, Black homeowners experienced an 80% increase in home values between

2014 and 2022—rising from $3.4 billion to $6.2 billion—contributing to generational wealth. And the poorest neighborhoods (primarily Hispanic and Latino) experienced the highest property value growth over the same period.

- **Young Talent Program.** Since 2015, over 79,680 young Detroit residents between the ages of 14 and 24 were given summer jobs, across a wide range of City of Detroit departments. By investing in the future of the city's youth, many from the program have gone on to start real careers, contributing to the health of the economy and improving economic mobility.[40]

- **Increase Financial Literacy to Improve Economic Mobility.** The Regional Chamber partnered with a non-profit organization, Operation Hope, to host centers where residents could come to increase their financial literacy by learning to manage personal finances, improve credit scores, and help make owning a home possible.[41]

These initiatives have helped Detroit, a city that was approaching economic disrepair, begin to thrive again. Because when leaders support their residents to find housing and work, educate themselves on financial literacy, and help them stay in their homes instead of being displaced—they give people the opportunity to be active, contributing members of the community and improves the potential for economic mobility. For residents who previously faced barriers keeping them stuck in one socioeconomic status, the potential for economic mobility uplifts not only the individuals themselves, but the entire community and city on a larger scale.

Let's now look again to Finland to see how they use equity to help support those without work.

REAL RESULTS FROM AROUND THE WORLD: FINLAND

What they do well: Finland continues to lead the way in equity around the world. This time, the country tested an unconditional basic income policy to promote social equity and improve employment outcomes, gaining global attention.

Key Equitable Initiative:

Basic Income Pilot: From 2017 to 2018, the country conducted a national, government-backed income experiment called the Ran Universal Basic Income pilot (UBI) where they paid 2,000 unemployed people a monthly income of 560 Euros for the year. This payment did not come with any requirements to find a job.

Benefits in Action:

The *Wellbeing Economy Alliance*—an organization committed to transforming the economic system— reported that this standardized monthly income in Finland actually led to more productivity among individuals. Guaranteed income meant that people could take temporary work or start businesses without the fear of losing benefits. Because basic necessities were met through this guaranteed monthly income, it "[freed] up time for people to pursue what they cared about." This led to increased satisfaction, less mental strain, and a more positive perception of their economic status.[42] This shows us that when people are able to improve their socioeconomic status, they can contribute more of their whole selves to the communities they live in.

WHEN EQUITY IS DONE RIGHT IN ECONOMIC INCLUSION

Just like in Chapter Eight, we're now going to turn the advantages for all when equity is done right. This time, we'll be looking at the global benefits through the lens of economic inclusion and what happens when we remove barriers to economic mobility.

Shared Advantages for Those in Both Groups | Stronger Communities + Moral and Economic Progress

We know from our discussions around equity in Part I and II of this book that equity aligns with principles of fairness and justice, both of which create societies that value all their members equally. Like we witnessed in Finland's unconditional income experiment, those without work were given the opportunity to be seen and included. When all members are valued on a level playing field and no one feels unheard or left out, it's possible for trust, collaboration, and social cohesion to grow across all groups. Let's take a look at how equity benefits both marginalized groups and majority groups in this way, fostering progress and stronger communities.

Advantages for Marginalized Groups | Reduction of Discrimination + Increased Representation

By addressing systemic inequities based on zip codes and socioeconomic status, equity helps reduce biases and discriminatory practices in society—and helps improve opportunities for economic mobility. We can see the real-world results of this through the equitable initiatives noted above from the U.S. and Finland. Both helped to better communities by providing tailored support to minority groups who have been negatively impacted by socioeconomic, racial, and other barriers that discouraged economic mobility.

Historically, we can also see how equity has reduced discrimination and increased representation of minority voices not only within economic mobility, but within workplaces, schools, and entire communities. Think of the Women's Suffrage or Civil Rights Movements in the United States, where minority groups (women and Black Americans) were once not allowed to vote. Not being able to vote was a form of discrimination that meant those groups' voices were not heard within the communities they lived in.

But when equitable progress levels the playing field, equal access to opportunities (like the right to vote, which both women and Black Americans now have), the outcome is representation that truly reflects the diversity within our communities. Equitable practices promote diversity in leadership, decision-making spaces, and peer spaces, ensuring all voices and perspectives are included.

Advantages for Those in the Majority | Enhanced Social Stability + Economic Growth

Societies with greater equity experience less social unrest, conflict, and economic friction, which benefits everyone. This truth has been seen time and time again. Why? Economic exclusion means that certain groups are left out of spaces, markets, and services, which negatively impacts the health of our individuals, communities, and the economy as a whole.

The health of our economy affects everyone, including those in the majority.

An example of this effect of exclusion is pay disparity. You'll remember the global gender pay gap we discussed in Chapter Three, where globally, women are paid less than men for the same job. *World Bank Group*—an international cooperative of 189 countries committed to ending poverty and boosting shared prosperity for all groups—estimates that gender inequality alone is responsible for the loss in human capital wealth of $160.2 trillion.[43] In other words, this gender pay gap negatively impacts the majority because it has a great impact on overall economic health when this lost human capital is not being reinfused into the economy as a whole.

But equity and inclusion have the opposite effect. For example, eliminating the gender pay gap through equitable practices leads to a greater positive impact for all. This is because equity *expands* opportunities for everyone to contribute to the economy, which leads to higher productivity and growth that benefits all members of society.

This is why it is so important for leaders to understand the varied issues people face that act as barriers to inclusion, representation, and economic mobility. Leaders need to recognize what those issues are—school systems in need of resources, access to affordable housing, and closing the pay gap. And they need to respect the different perspectives and starting points of their communities in order for all to reap the benefits of equity done right.

When we include all perspectives in community initiatives and ask—*What strategies do we need to put into place so that everyone is heard?*—that is how we bring up all neighborhoods economically and provide greater opportunities for economic mobility for the people within them. When we do that, the entire city can function better. City-wide equitable initiatives ensure everyone is better represented, and consumers spend accordingly. The crime rate decreases because all groups have what they need, and no one group is functioning in survival mode. Social structures and a sense of community build among the society as a whole.

Because when both those in the minority and those in the majority can exist in a state of social balance (where a diverse community functions with understanding, trust, and economic balance among neighbors), disruption to the social order decreases. That is the power of equity.

CHAPTER TEN

EQUITY IN ACTION | WORKPLACE AND TEAMS

One thing to know about me, I have terrible allergies—dog dander, mold, pollen, plants, *everything*. They're so bad that when my children were little, they used to say that I was allergic to the outside. A few years back, there was one season when my allergies got so bad that my eyes became so red, swollen, and itchy that it looked like I'd been punched—in both eyes. This particular allergy season taught me a huge lesson in equity. Let me explain further.

Some days, my allergies and swollen face would keep me from going to work. My sinuses would take such a beating, my throat, nose, and ears were so blocked that it affected my hearing.

On days when I was struggling, but still made it into the office, I remember being incredibly embarrassed because I continuously had to ask coworkers, *"I'm sorry, what did you say? Could you repeat that a bit louder?"* because I couldn't hear them through my blocked sinuses. Finally, I knew I had to do something to adapt with my limited hearing ability thanks to my allergies.

So I did some research on tools that were available for people who were hard of hearing to help assist me during this particularly bad allergy season. I found a speaker device that was specifically designed to connect to my laptop. Instead of using the computer speaker, this device actually amplified the sound so I could hear better during online meetings. Thankfully, with the help of this device, I didn't have to ask, *"I'm sorry, could you please speak up?"* a single time after that.

Now, you may be wondering what this has to do with equity. But it has so much to do with equity.

Because devices like the one that hooked up to my laptop to help me hear better during a time of need, or similarly, speech-to-text programs like Google Assistant or Otter. ai, that we all now benefit from at work, were originally born from a software designed as an equitable solution for individuals with physical or learning disabilities.

This is one of the clearest ways I know of to exemplify what I mean when I say *we all benefit when equity is done right*. Because, while yes, acts of equity can be big like policy changes or nationwide programs—like those we saw in the last two chapters—equity also exists in smaller ways, like products or services developed and built for those who need accommodation to work and thrive on a level playing field.

Something as simple and normal as allergies meant *I* needed a more level playing field for a few months, and I found one by being resourceful and looking for a device that helps give equal opportunity to engage in the workplace to those who are hard of hearing. Likewise, there have been numerous equitable devices for individuals with physical or learning disabilities, mobility impairments, or visual impairments who often face a barrier to traditional typing or computer use. Let's take a better look at this by exploring speech-to-text programs.

EQUITY IN PRODUCTS AND SERVICES

Otherwise known as voice dictation, speech-to-text functionality, was developed as an assistive technology to help people with disabilities write, learn, and communicate independently.

In other words, these tools were designed to help level the playing field for our disabled peers by giving them resources tailored to their unique needs and allowed them to listen, write, speak, and most importantly, participate in workplace and school settings on more equal footing with their non-disabled peers. These early voice-recognition systems, like IBM's Shoebox, which led to more robust programs like ViaVoice or Dragon NaturallySpeaking, enabled users to dictate documents, control operating systems, and compose messages entirely by speaking. They granted unprecedented independence, empowered disabled individuals to fully participate in education, employment, and public life.

Today, however, speech-to-text communication has become a widely adopted feature in homes, offices, and classrooms around the world. Although it was designed to give access, it is now a universal productivity tool that we all benefit from. And if you're anything like me and my family, you use it almost daily.

"Alexa, what's the weather like today?" "Siri, play my workout playlist?" "Google Maps, how do I get home from my current location?"

Sound familiar? What was once considered assistive technology has evolved into a core feature in everyday devices like our cell phones, laptops, gaming devices, GPS, and workplace tools.

Now, professionals across industries use voice dictation to increase efficiency by:

- Writing emails, reports, and notes faster than typing.
- Capturing ideas during commutes or while multi-tasking.
- Reducing hand and wrist strain from prolonged keyboard use.
- Transcribing meetings and interviews in real time.

Popular tools include built-in dictation features in Microsoft Word and Google Docs, virtual assistants like Google Assistant, and dedicated transcription apps such as Otter.ai and Fathom. These tools are now standard in most operating systems and productivity suites, and they allow us all to work more efficiently, at a faster pace. They accommodate our varying needs when we are temporarily on the go, or under the weather, like I was during that particularly bad allergy season.

We use speech-to-text software in our personal lives too, for things like:

- Supporting language learning, like Duolingo, or using translation devices for multilingual users during travel and personal day-to-day activities.
- Making Instagram/TikTok reels, television, and movies more accessible through real-time captions and transcripts.
- Using Google Maps, Apple Maps, or Waze to navigate someplace new, and getting turn-by-turn directions from the GPS voice software.
- And so much more.

Speech-to-text software is just one example to help us illustrate the broader benefits of designing products, services, policies, and practices with equity in mind. The next time you think that equity in action doesn't benefit everyone, just think about the last time you asked Siri or Alexa for something. And remember, when one group is uplifted, we *all* benefit.

To see these equitable benefits in action, let's now look at employment equity in action in Canada and Spain.

REAL RESULTS FROM AROUND THE WORLD: CANADA

Key Equitable Initiatives:

- **Employment Equity Act (1986)** – Canada requires federally regulated employers to remove workplace barriers for four designated groups: women, Indigenous peoples, persons with disabilities, and visible minorities. The *Canadian Human Rights Commission* tells us that this act is intended to "ensure that everyone in Canada has the same access to the labour market." Further, employers are required to "investigate, identify, and take concrete action to correct the conditions of disadvantage in employment." In order to do so, training is provided to employers in things like workforce analysis, employment systems reviews, employment equity plans, annual reports, and more to ensure equity in the workplace is upheld, and no one group is left out or underserved.[44]

- **Pay Equity Act (2018)** – This act aims to ensure equal pay for work of equal value, especially in federally regulated workplaces. This act intends to address and correct the gender pay gap in Canada (a pay gap that we know exists globally from our discussion in Chapter Three). Employers must establish a "pay equity plan" that compares the compensation between "predominantly female and male job classes doing work of equal or comparable value."[45] In other words, employers must have an equity pay plan that ensures they are paying male and female employees equal amounts for work of comparable value. And for any areas where female job classes are found to be underpaid compared to their male counterparts, employers must issue pay increases over three years, closing the gender pay gap within that company.

Benefits in Action:
These equitable policies and practices in Canada help to build a more representative workforce by removing

systemic barriers and requiring inclusion of minority groups to level the playing field. This ensures that workplaces more accurately reflect the diversity of Canadian society.

Through structured training and accountability (like workforce analysis and annual reports), Canadian organizations embed equity into their hiring, promotion, pay, and retention practices. Closing the gender pay gap ensures everyone is paid fairly and equitably, boosting financial independence and economic justice for citizens. This effectively leads to long-term cultural change for all, fostering inclusive workplaces where no one is left out or underserved.

Now let's take a look at how Spain works to provide equitable opportunities in the workplace for new parents.

REAL RESULTS FROM AROUND THE WORLD: SPAIN

Key Equitable Initiatives:[46]

The first six weeks after a child is born, paid leave is mandatory in Spain to support families as they adjust.

To further support families raising children, in 2024, Spain entitled all parents to 16 weeks of paid parental leave, meaning households with two parents became eligible to take up to 32 weeks of paid leave.

However, because this meant that single-family households were only eligible for 16 weeks of paid parental leave, the Superior Court of Justice recently ruled that this policy was discriminatory to single parents, since they received half of the time off with the same needs (to care for their children) as a two-parent household. This ruling is intended to grant single-parent families the same amount of leave as two-parent families (26 – 32 weeks).

Benefits in Action:

Today, parents in Spain are able to take the time off work that they need to care for their children *without* risking losing income or job standing as a result. This equitable policy also applies to self-employed workers, not only those who are employed by a company.

Further, as *Employee Benefits*, a human resources publication, tells us—because women tend to lead single-parent families, these measures are intended to provide "equality of treatment and opportunities between women and men in employment and occupation," helping to bridge the gender gap that impacts working women.

WHEN EQUITY IS DONE RIGHT IN THE WORKPLACE

Just like in Chapters Eight and Nine, we're now going to look at the advantages for all when equity is done right. In this section, we'll be looking at the global benefits for all, through the lens of equity in the workplace.

Shared Advantages for Those in Both Groups | Better Decision-Making

Diverse perspectives in the workplace result in more comprehensive and inclusive decisions. We know from Chapter Seven that when equity is intentionally incorporated into the workplace, we can leverage the inherent diversity of our world. Only when this diversity is leveraged optimally can we build a culture of inclusion where everyone can contribute fully to the entire team.

We saw the real-world effects of this advantage when we looked at how diverse teams actually outperform non-diverse teams in the long run.

Further, equity in teams and leaders can also be translated to politics, where leaders make more effective change when they speak for the entirety of the population they serve, not only one group. When diverse individuals come together in an equitable environment where everyone is welcomed to be heard, better decision-making is possible.

Advantages for Marginalized Groups | Access to Opportunities

Equity removes systemic barriers, enabling individuals to access education, employment, and other resources tailored to their needs. Workplace equity and our examples from Spain and Canada above show us how powerful it is when people are afforded access to opportunities, especially those who have historically been underserved or excluded by systems not built with them in mind. When we prioritize equity, it means systemic barriers (like the gender pay gap) are not only identified but actively dismantled and then rebuilt in a way that opens opportunities for all.

Some opportunity-making acts of equity include: mentorship programs and career development opportunities that are tailored to marginalized employees' unique starting points and life circumstances. These acts of equity are not about giving an unfair advantage. They're about giving everyone equal access to opportunities.

For marginalized groups, this access can be life-changing—opening pathways to leadership, education, and economic mobility, to name just a few. Remember, when people from underrepresented backgrounds are supported, the ripple effect goes beyond individual success, by giving the entire community the valuable insights, perspectives, and value we did not have before.

Advantages for Those in the Majority | Fairer Workplaces and Communities + Increased Innovation and Creativity

Equity doesn't just level the playing field for marginalized groups—it creates fairer, more functional environments for those in the majority as well. When organizations commit to equitable systems, they reduce favoritism, bias, and exclusion for all, creating a workplace culture where merit is more easily recognized and rewarded. In other words, equitable systems help us work towards true merit-based recognition, where everyone can be celebrated on the basis of merit alone (which we spoke about in great detail in Chapter Five).

Further, equity in the workplace is a powerful engine for innovation. Diverse teams, when given equitable opportunities to contribute, foster innovation as they generate more creative ideas and solutions. Capitalizing on fresh insights adds value to any team within organizations that seek to understand their workforce, the market and their customers. Whether it's designing a product, launching a service, or solving a complex challenge, having a range of perspectives at the table leads to stronger, more sustainable outcomes. For those in the majority, this means being a part of workplaces that are better positioned to grow, adapt, and thrive in the modern world.

WE ALL WIN

We have discussed at great length the misunderstandings around equity, diving into what the word is and what it isn't. But now, in wrapping up Part III, we've also spoken about the *benefits*. I'm sure at one point (or perhaps many points) throughout this book, I have challenged your preexisting beliefs and offered you a new perspective.

Perhaps you never thought about the benefits that exist when we get equity right—such as equity in the workplace, and in education and healthcare. Benefits of economic opportunity and mobility are not only for marginalized communities, but for everyone. And yes, everyone in this case—no matter the color of your skin, your gender, your job, your experiences, opportunities, or setbacks— includes you.

When we get it right, equity has the power to benefit us all. That is something I believe should be celebrated. So, as we wrap up this section and this book, let us celebrate the potential that small and large acts of equity have to help us all see over the fence. Let us celebrate the potential for the day when that fence is torn down, and we can all play this game called life on an equal playing field.

The possibilities that await us in this more equitable future are something I believe, with my whole heart, that each and every one of us should get to see.

CHAPTER ELEVEN

THE POWER TO LEAD OURSELVES, YOUR ROLE IN GETTING EQUITY RIGHT

Although I will forever call on our leaders, governments, large public and private corporations, and educational institutions to enact equity into their policies, equity can, and should, exist on a more personal scale as well.

That is where you come in.

We know from Chapter Seven just how important inclusion is. There is much strength and benefit to be had by actively creating spaces where all can participate, when we all can be a part of the equation. That's why I want to continue the celebration of equity we spoke about at the end of Chapter Ten by ensuring that you feel fully <u>included</u> in the work and encouraging you to be a part of the change.

You may be thinking—*okay, this is all great, but I don't know if I'm brave enough, confident enough, or bold enough to use my voice to speak out. I'm not a change-maker.*

Maybe there have been instances where you feel you've misstepped before that are making you feel this way now.

When you didn't stand up for someone being marginalized, and you wish you had. Maybe there have been times when you didn't stand up for *yourself*. I encourage you not to use these cases as proof that you do not have it in you to speak up for change. Instead, I want you to give yourself grace, because you did the best you could with the knowledge and tools that you had at the time.

I invite you to hold the famous quote by Maya Angelou, American poet and civil rights activist, near and dear whenever your voice threatens to shake: *"Do the best you can until you know better. Then, when you know better, do better."*

Now that you've read this book, you have so much more information and knowledge to do better the next time you're presented with an opportunity to speak up. Whether you're a team leader yourself, a working professional, a stay-at-home parent, a retiree, or a student—we all have the power to lead ourselves.

Trust me, you have that spark of leadership within you already. And the change you make does not need to be loud. Instead, it can be through simple individual actions you take every day as that self-leader to promote equity and encourage others to do so as well.

INDIVIDUAL ACTIONS YOU CAN TAKE DAILY

In this section, let's explore some of my favorite, simplest, and least scary ways to speak up for equity. So that, if you feel called, you can do your part to hold the vision of equity—and help create a more beautiful future for everyone.

Awareness and Education

By reading this book, you have taken the first step in building your knowledge about equity. But I encourage you not to stop here. Continue to read, build your education and awareness, and then act upon it.

You can use your newfound equity knowledge to better your own life. Like my example from living in Jacksonville, Florida, use your knowledge as a tool to enrich your own opportunities. When you move to a new city or to a new neighborhood within your current community, be more assertive in your housing choices. Study the city before you reach out to the real estate agent, do your own research around what neighborhoods you'd like to live in, and do not let anyone (or any system) lead you.

Instead, lead yourself.

This self-leadership can be applied not only in your choice of neighborhood, but in your workplace, in your social life, in your family dynamics... the list goes on. You can advocate for personal rocks of equity in every area of your life, and I think that you absolutely should. Because when we better ourselves and advocate for our own opportunities, we enrich the spaces we exist in. We show up as better, more holistic versions of ourselves who speak up for our own needs and champion our own growth.

Advocacy and Policy Changes

I often get asked: *"But Celeste, what if I'm not in a leadership position? What if I don't have the responsibility of writing policy? What can I do?"*

The fact of the matter is that most of us aren't in direct positions of power, whether that be politically, within the workplace, or in education. We see inequities play themselves out day after day and can feel paralyzed to do anything about them because we do not directly write or implement policy. But for the individual person who isn't in a job or position where you have the responsibility of writing policy to make equitable change on an institutional level, don't be discouraged. You still have power—and there is so much you can do with it.

One of the best ways you can advocate for equitable change is through the political system. Take part, and exercise your right to have your voice heard.

The first step? Use your voice by voting. Advocacy can be as simple as getting out to the ballot box. Yes, we've all been told to exercise our right to vote, and it may feel like a broken record for me to tell you again now, but you'd be surprised by just how many people don't show up to make their voice heard—whether at the local, state, or country-wide level. You don't just vote on people, you vote on bills, policies, and local initiatives as well.

In other words, you vote on *equity*. So, use the political system to advocate for different policies that are going to have an impact.

Likewise, even if you don't directly write policy, you absolutely still have the power to *influence*. Political leaders are elected to be the voice of the people, to serve the people. But in order to do that well, each and every voice needs to be heard; so get loud! Write your local leaders, your state leaders, global leaders, and politicians. Let them know what's needed in your community, and *for* your community. Support policies that address systemic barriers (like affordable healthcare and accessible education). And don't be afraid to tell those leaders, who do write policy, what you think and what you *need.*

Other Individual Actions

We all know the phrase, "If You See Something, Say Something®," thanks to the national campaign from Homeland Security in the United States.[47] If you've traveled anywhere in the U.S., you know that the phrase is on posters lining almost every wall, blasted over the loudspeaker, and uttered countless times a day at our airports, bus stations, and train stations.

It reminds you to recognize the signs of any suspicious behavior and to report anything that unsettles you. It's easy to remember and easy to take action.

This may be a strange comparison, but I like to say that we can all play a similar role here when it comes to equity. If you see inequity playing out, don't be afraid to speak up. It is perhaps the simplest, but most effective, individual action you can take daily.

When you see something—someone being treated inequitably, someone treating you inequitably—say something. In your community, at your job, on your college campus, in your family unit—no space is too small or insignificant to become an equitable one.

Other simple, individual actions include: listening to others' experiences, challenging biases, and advocating for those at a disadvantage. If you're up to the task, you may also be a source of education for others to learn about systemic issues and privilege by speaking up about what equity is and what it isn't. If you don't feel comfortable speaking up and speaking out in a particular situation or with a specific person, that's okay too—hand them a copy of this book, and let them make their own choices with the same knowledge you now have.

When we focus on equity, we create stronger spaces where everyone can prosper and feel good about their lives. My hope is that anyone you pass this book along to will become an active ally of change after they, too, are let in on the truth about equity—what it is, what it isn't, and why we all win when we get it right.

YOUR ROLE IN GETTING EQUITY RIGHT

I want to return now, to the quote at the very beginning of this book, so that you may revisit it with new context, with fresh eyes, and equipped with all of the knowledge and tools around equity you now hold.

"Equity is not a destination—it's a commitment and a daily choice. We each hold the power to challenge inequity and uplift those who have been excluded. We don't need to wait for perfect systems, we just need to begin with imperfect courage. The time to act is now, and the responsibility is ours."

With this sentiment in mind, I hope that you choose to take up this mantle of responsibility.

Begin. Then begin again every time your awareness helps you learn something new.

Act. With courage—and then act again, and again.

Move. Take small steps forward, even when big leaps feel impossible.

EQUITY IS HOW WE MOVE FORWARD, TOGETHER

Although this may be the end of our journey through these pages together, it is just the beginning of our collective journey to ensure that everyone has the rocks of equity they need to succeed—to be the catalyst of change, *while* we do the more long term work of tearing down the fence. I believe that when we fail to prioritize equity—when Diversity, Equity, and Inclusion efforts are dismissed, watered-down, or halted altogether—the costs are steep and far-reaching. Because just as equity benefits us all, inequity has long-lasting negative impacts.

We know from our deep and varied discussions throughout this book that inequity widens disparities by shutting out marginalized groups, keeping them from equal opportunities, and limiting their ability to contribute and thrive. We also know that innovation stalls in homogeneous environments, and organizations miss out on the insights and creativity that come from diverse teams.

Likewise, trust in institutions erodes when people see systems they perceive as unfair, systems that benefit the few while excluding many. In these workplaces, inequity drives burnout, employee turnover, and disengagement— especially among those who are already underrepresented. This limits growth, adaptability, and resilience company-wide.

Further, the ripple effect of inequity extends far beyond our workplaces. In broader communities and societies, a lack of equity can fuel tensions, protests, and conflict, as groups demand justice and reform. In other words, inequity not only breeds social and political instability but also legal and reputational risks as well. By failing to uphold equitable practices and by leaving any one group out of the conversation, private companies and government institutions alike face lawsuits, cancel culture (when a company is shunned or boycotted for acting in an unacceptable, non-inclusive, manner), and reputational damage—which can be incredibly hard to repair.

That's why equity isn't just the ethical or moral thing to do—it's the smart thing to do, it's the logical thing to do. When everyone has access to equal opportunities, we unlock our full social, political, and economic potential. Imagine what's possible when we invest our efforts into bringing *everyone* up instead of holding anyone back. We strengthen our schools, our institutions, our businesses, and our democracies. Our economies thrive, our societies thrive, and our political systems speak for *everyone*.

When we get equity right, we cultivate innovation, boost performance, and create the conditions for all people to thrive. Equity is how we build a future where barriers are dismantled, talent is given permission to soar, and prosperity is truly shared by all.

Equity is how we move forward, *together.*

As we close out this book, remember: equity is not just a policy or a program—it is deeply personal. It lives in the choices we make every day, in how we listen, how we lead, and how we stand up when it would be easier to stay silent. Progress may be slow, but it is built one person, one action, and one moment of courage at a time.

We all have a role to play in getting equity right. My hope is that you'll play it.

RESOURCES

OTHER BOOKS BY THE AUTHOR

How to Be a Diversity and Inclusion Ambassador: Everyone's Role in Helping All Feel Accepted, Engaged, and Valued

GET IN TOUCH

If you'd like to connect with the author for a speaking or consulting opportunity, or regarding questions about her books, get in touch via her website https://www.crwdiversity.com/.

ENDNOTES

1. Christy C. Bulkeley, "A Pioneering Generation Marked the Path for Women Journalists," *Nieman Reports*, March 15, 2002, https://niemanreports.org/a-pioneering-generation-marked-the-path-for-women-journalists/.

2. Juliet Bourke and Bernadette Dillon, "*The Diversity and Inclusion Revolution*," *Deloitte Review*, no. 22 (January 2018): 90, fig. 7, "Equality vs. Equity in the Short- and Long-Term." Accessed May 25, 2025. https://www2.deloitte.com/content/dam/insights/us/articles/4209_Diversity-and-inclusion-revolution/DI_Diversity-and-inclusion-revolution.pdf.

3. Joseph R. Biden Jr., *Advancing Racial Equity and Support for Underserved Communities Through the Federal Government*, Executive Order 13985, January 20, 2021, Federal Register 86, no. 14 (January 25, 2021): 7009–7013, https://www.federalregister.gov/documents/2021/01/25/2021-01753/advancing-racial-equity-and-support-for-underserved-communities-through-the-federal-government.

4. Council of Europe Parliamentary Assembly, *Ethnic Profiling: A Rising Trend in Europe*, Provisional Version, November 27, 2020, https://assembly.coe.int/LifeRay/EGA/Pdf/TextesProvisoires/2020/20201127-EthnicProfiling-EN.pdf.

5. Ayanna Alexander, "Trump and Other Republicans Want to Roll Back DEI Programs in Education. They Say It's Discrimination," *AP News*, March 21, 2024, https://apnews.com/article/trump-dei-education-diversity-equity-inclusion-20cf8a2941f4f35e0b5b0e07c6347ebb.

6. American Association for Access, Equity, and Diversity. "About Affirmative Action, Diversity and Inclusion." *AAAED*. Accessed April 12, 2025. https://www.aaaed.org/aaaed/About_Affirmative_Action_Diversity_and_Inclusion.asp.

7. Equal Pay Today. "Gender Pay Gap Statistics 2025: A Comprehensive Analysis," *Equal Pay Today*, March 18, 2025, https://www.equalpaytoday.org/gender-pay-gap-statistics/.

8. Kweilin Ellingrud, "New Demographic Reality Poses Challenges for Countries and Companies," Forbes, February 13, 2025, https://www.forbes.com/sites/kweilinellingrud/2025/02/13/new-demographic-reality-poses-challenges-for-countries-and-companies/.

9. USAging, *2025 Policy Priorities*, March 2025, https://www.usaging.org/Files/USAging_2025PolicyPriorities_final_WEB%20%281%29.pdf.

10. Congressional Budget Office, *The Demographic Outlook: 2025 to 2055*, January 13, 2025, https://www.cbo.gov/publication/60875.

11. A.W. Geiger and Sarah Naseer, "Key Facts About Women's Suffrage Around the World, a Century After U.S. Ratified 19th Amendment," *Pew Research Center*, October 5, 2020, https://www.pewresearch.org/short-reads/2020/10/05/key-facts-about-womens-suffrage-around-the-world-a-century-after-u-s-ratified-19th-amendment/.

12. Human Rights Campaign, "Marriage Equality Around the World," *Human Rights Campaign*, accessed April 21, 2025, https://www.hrc.org/resources/marriage-equality-around-the-world.

13. William H. Frey, *Diversity Explosion: How New Racial Demographics Are Remaking America* (Washington, D.C.: Brookings Institution Press, 2015).

14. William H. Frey, "The U.S. Will Become 'Minority White' in 2045, Census Projects," *Brookings*, March 14, 2018, https://www.brookings.edu/articles/the-us-will-become-minority-white-in-2045-census-projects/.

15. D'Vera Cohn, Jeffrey S. Passel, and Ana Gonzalez-Barrera, "Future Immigration Will Change the Face of America by 2065," *Pew Research Center*, October 5, 2015, https://www.pewresearch.org/short-reads/2015/10/05/future-immigration-will-change-the-face-of-america-by-2065/.

16. UK '40% Ethnic Minorities by 2050," *Belfast Telegraph*, May 2, 2013, https://www.belfasttelegraph.co.uk/news/uk-40-ethnic-minorities-by-2050/29237617.html.

17. World Population Review, "Caucasian Countries 2024." Accessed May 5, 2025. https://worldpopulationreview.com/country-rankings/caucasian-countries.

18. BBC News, "Should we drop ethnic minority for global majority?," *BBC News*, October 20, 2024, https://www.bbc.co.uk/news/articles/c981g43vmmro.

19. Rosemary Campbell-Stephens, "Global Majority Leadership," *Rosemary Campbell-Stephens*, accessed April 20, 2025, https://rosemarycampbellstephens.com/global-majority-leadership/.

20. The Diversity Movement, "Genuine v. Performative: How to Be Sure Your DEI Efforts Are Authentic," *Jamie Ousterout,* January 6, 2022, https://thediversitymovement.com/genuine-performative-how-to-be-sure-dei-efforts-are-authentic/.

21. Beyond Performative DEI: How Companies Can Foster True Inclusion," Diversity.com, January 22, 2025, diversity.com/post/beyond-performative-dei-true-inclusion.

22. How Blind Auditions Help Orchestras to Eliminate Gender Bias," *The Guardian*, October 14, 2013, https://www.theguardian.com/women-in-leadership/2013/oct/14/blind-auditions-orchestras-gender-bias.

23. "Disparate Impact Under Fire: What EO 14281 Means for Equal Opportunity," Potomac Law, May 5, 2025, https://www.potomaclaw.com/news-Disparate-Impact-Under-Fire.

24. "Griggs v. Duke Power Co.," *Encyclopedia Britannica*, accessed May 5, 2025, https://www.britannica.com/event/Griggs-v-Duke-Power-Co.

25. U.S. Equal Employment Opportunity Commission, *Title VII of the Civil Rights Act of 1964*, accessed May 5, 2025, https://www.eeoc.gov/statutes/title-vii-civil-rights-act-1964#:~:text=Title%20VII%20prohibits%20employment%20discrimination,religion%2C%20sex%20and%20national%20origin.

26. U.S. Equal Employment Opportunity Commission, *Who Is Protected from Employment Discrimination?* Accessed May 5, 2025, https://www.eeoc.gov/employers/small-business/3-who-protected-employment-discrimination#:~:text=Applicants%2C%20employees%20and%20former%20employees,(including%20family%20medical%20history).

27. Nadine Jolie Courtney, "These Preschools Are the Ivy League of Early Education," *Town & Country*, October 11, 2016, https://www.townandcountrymag.com/society/a7811/best-preschools/.

28. There Is Only So Much We Can Do – School Staff in England," Child Poverty Action Group, September 19, 2023, https://cpag.org.uk/news/there-only-so-much-we-can-do-school-staff-england.

29. Mind Tools Content Team, "Forming, Storming, Norming, and Performing: Understanding the Stages of Team Formation," *Mind Tools*. Accessed May 13, 2025, https://www.mindtools.com/abyj5fi/forming-storming-norming-and-performing.

30. Hunt, Vivian, Sara Prince, Kevin Dolan, and Lareina Yee. *Diversity Matters Even More: The Case for Holistic Impact.* McKinsey & Company, October 4, 2023, https://www.mckinsey.com/featured-insights/diversity-and-inclusion/diversity-matters-even-more-the-case-for-holistic-impact.

31. Lorenzo, Rocío, Nicole Voigt, Karin Schetelig, Annika Zawadzki, Isabell M. Welpe, and Philipp Gerbert. *How Diverse Leadership Teams Boost Innovation.* Boston Consulting Group, January 23, 2018, https://www.bcg.com/publications/2018/how-diverse-leadership-teams-boost-innovation.

32. Erik Larson, "New Research: Diversity + Inclusion = Better Decision Making at Work," *Forbes*, September 21, 2017, https://www.

forbes.com/sites/eriklarson/2017/09/21/new-research-diversity-inclusion-better-decision-making-at-work/.

33. Sean A.P. Clouston, Douglas W. Hanes, and Bruce G. Link, "Social Inequalities and the Early Provision and Dispersal of COVID-19 Vaccinations in the United States: A Population Trends Study," *Health Affairs* 43, no. 1 (July 16, 2023), https://pmc.ncbi.nlm.nih.gov/articles/PMC10723195.

34. EJ_Editor. "Leading the Way in Education: Finland's Focus on Innovation and Equity." *Education Journalist*, January 17, 2025, https://educationjournalist.com/leading-the-way-in-education-finlands-focus-on-innovation-and-equity/.

35. Indigenous Services Canada. "Jordan's Principle." *Government of Canada*, last modified March 10, 2025, https://www.sac-isc.gc.ca/eng/1568396042341/1568396159824.

36. Riley McLaughlin, "The Importance of Culturally Competent Care," *The Mosaic Institute*, December 5, 2022, https://www.mosaicinstitute.ca/post/the-importance-of-culturally-competent-care.

37. Canadian Virtual Hospice. "Culture." *Living My Culture*. Accessed May 22, 2025, https://livingmyculture.ca/culture/.

38. Kieran Chidi Nduagbo, "How Gender Disparities Affect Classroom Learning," *ASCD*, July 23, 2020, https://www.ascd.org/el/articles/how-gender-disparities-affect-classroom-learning.

39. Associated Press, "Home Values Rising in Detroit, Especially for Black Homeowners, Study Shows," *AP News*, April 16, 2024, https://apnews.com/article/detroit-home-values-bankruptcy-duggan-27a057984970f3fb2359ce41a43908cc.AP News.

40. City of Detroit, "Detroit Youth Begin Signing Up for 8,000+ Summer Jobs as Mayor Mike Duggan Opens 2025 GDYT Application Portal," February 6, 2025, https://detroitmi.gov/news/detroit-youth-begin-signing-8000-summer-jobs-mayor-mike-duggan-opens-2025-gdyt-application-portal.

41. Sandy Baruah and Mark Davidoff, "Economic Inclusion Must Top Priority List," *The Detroit News*, October 29, 2015, https://

eu.detroitnews.com/story/opinion/2015/10/29/baruah-davidoff-economic-inclusion/74775518/.

42. Wellbeing Economy Alliance. "Finland – Universal Basic Income Pilot." *Wellbeing Economy Alliance.* Accessed May 23, 2025. https://weall.org/resource/finland-universal-basic-income-pilot.Wellbeing Economy Alliance+5Wellbeing Economy Alliance+5Wellbeing Economy Alliance+5.

43. World Bank. "Social Inclusion." *World Bank.* Accessed May 24, 2025. https://www.worldbank.org/en/topic/social-inclusion.

44. Canadian Human Rights Commission, "Employment Equity." Accessed May 26, 2025. https://www.chrc-ccdp.gc.ca/individuals/employment-equity.

45. Employment and Social Development Canada, "Overview of the Pay Equity Act," *Canada.ca*, last modified November 28, 2023, https://www.canada.ca/en/services/jobs/workplace/human-rights/overview-pay-equity-act.html.

46. Spain to Allow Single Parents to Take Double Parental Leave," *Employee Benefits*, accessed May 26, 2025, https://employeebenefits.co.uk/benefits-for-carers/spain-to-allow-single-parents-to-take-double-parental-leave/279993.article.

47. U.S. Department of Homeland Security, "About the 'If You See Something, Say Something®' Campaign," accessed May 27, 2025, https://www.dhs.gov/see-something-say-something/about-campaign.

ABOUT THE AUTHOR

Celeste Warren is a trailblazing voice in the global movement for diversity, equity, and inclusion.

With nearly four decades of leadership at major corporations—including a decade as Chief Diversity and Inclusion Officer—Celeste has devoted her career to transforming workplace cultures and opening doors of opportunity for all. Now, as the founder of Celeste Warren Consulting, LLC, she partners with organizations to build inclusive environments where every individual feels seen, heard, and valued.

A dynamic speaker and acclaimed author, Celeste's groundbreaking work has inspired leaders across the world to turn intention into action. Her passion, wisdom, and lived experience shine through every page of this book—urging readers to become powerful agents of change in their communities and companies.

www.ingramcontent.com/pod-product-compliance
Lightning Source LLC
Chambersburg PA
CBHW060226030426
42335CB00014B/1353